Governors State University
Library
Hours:
Monday thru Thursday 8:30 to 10:30
Friday and Saturday 8:30 to 5:00
Sunday 1:00 to 5:00 (Fall and Winter Trimester Only)

DEMCO

COUNSELING SKILLS
SKILLS
for
TEACHERS

second edition

COUNSELING
SKILLS
for
TEACHERS

second edition

Jeffrey A. Kottler
Ellen Kottler

CORWIN PRESS
A SAGE Publications Company
Thousand Oaks, CA 91320

For information:

Corwin Press
A Sage Publications Company
2455 Teller Road
Thousand Oaks, California 91320
www.corwinpress.com

Sage Publications Ltd.
1 Oliver's Yard
55 City Road
London EC1Y 1SP
United Kingdom

Sage Publications India Pvt. Ltd.
B-42, Panchsheel Enclave
Post Box 4109
New Delhi 110 017 India

Printed in the United States of America

Library of Congress Cataloging-in-Publication Data

Kottler, Jeffrey A.
Counseling skills for teachers / Jeffrey A. Kottler, Ellen Kottler. — 2nd ed.
    p. cm.
Includes bibliographical references and index.
ISBN 1-4129-4921-1 or 978-1-4129-4921-7 (cloth)
ISBN 1-4129-4922-X or 978-1-4129-4922-4 (pbk.)
    1. Teacher participation in educational counseling—United States. 2. Teacher-student relationships—United States. I. Kottler, Ellen. II. Title.
LB1027.5.K663 2007
371.4'046—dc22

                                        2006017033

This book is printed on acid-free paper.

06   07   08   09   10   10   9   8   7   6   5   4   3   2   1

Acquisitions Editor:	Stacy Wagner
Editorial Assistant:	Joanna Coelho
Production Editor:	Melanie Birdsall
Copy Editor:	Brenda Weight
Typesetter:	C&M Digitals (P) Ltd.
Proofreader:	Kristin Bergstad
Indexer:	Michael Ferreira
Cover Designer:	Scott Van Atta

Contents

Preface

Modern-day teachers, by necessity, do much more than present content and information to children. In fact, actual time spent lecturing represents less than half of the teacher's daily responsibilities. In addition to time in front of a classroom, you may be expected during a typical day to break up a fight; console a child whose feelings have been hurt; help a student resolve a personal problem; lead a heated discussion about a provocative issue; meet with a distraught parent; explain to two kids why their continued feud is not in their best interests; and offer comfort to a variety of others who are feeling sad, lonely, anxious, frustrated, angry, or depressed.

This reality is especially ironic considering the amount of time that teacher education programs spend on helping educators become experts in their content areas and proficient in the materials, methods, and management of pedagogical presentations. Although this training will indeed serve you well, you will often feel way over your head dealing with personal/interpersonal problems that you may never have anticipated.

In addition to their duties and responsibilities as classroom managers, teachers are called on to do a variety of things for which they may feel unprepared, such as the following:

1. Respond to children's emotional needs

2. Resolve personal conflicts and settle fights

3. Serve as surrogate parents and mentors for children who lack positive role models

4. Act as confidantes to students who are struggling with personal issues

5. Identify children suffering from abuse, neglect, drug abuse, and a variety of emotional problems, and make appropriate referrals when necessary

6. Assess children's developmental transitions and guide their continued physical, emotional, social, and spiritual growth, in addition to their cognitive development

7. Lead discussions dealing with an assortment of emotional and personal issues

8. Participate in individualized education programs (IEPs)

9. Conduct parent conferences on the phone and in person

10. Function as problem solvers for those children in the throes of crisis

In short, even though they may have had precious little training in these specialties, teachers are often required to use a variety of counseling skills. They do this not only during planned interactions for which students and parents schedule meetings, but more often in the hallways, on playgrounds, during extracurricular functions, and in the classroom when lessons are taking place.

The intent of this book is *not* to equip teachers with the background or the skills to function in the role of a counselor or human relations consultant—that is what school counselors, psychologists, and social workers do. The reality of daily school life, however, is that teachers must often serve in helping roles beyond their responsibilities as content experts. As you stand before your classes talking about history or grammar, you cannot help but notice the children who seem tired or lonely or troubled. As you sit at your desk grading papers, you will be visited by children who trust you, children who want someone to listen to them and understand them. As you speak with parents or other colleagues about children in your charge, you will be required to demonstrate a high degree of interpersonal sensitivity and skill.

It is our hope, therefore, that this book will introduce you to the basic methodology of counseling skills. Although we cannot make a counselor out of a teacher in a format as limited as this (years of supervised practice are needed), we certainly can sensitize educators to the basic ideas and skills that are involved in responding to students' interpersonal, social, and emotional needs.

NEW FOR THE SECOND EDITION

In the second edition of this book, we have completely updated the content, focusing on several contemporary issues related to homelessness, dealing with grief and loss issues, confronting bullying and harassment, and motivating students who are disengaged. We have also considerably expanded the chapter on counseling in groups to describe many ways that the skills you learn can be used in the classroom to build a culture of respect and tolerance.

In addition, we have added a new chapter. "Counseling Yourself" focuses on ways that both new and veteran teachers can take care of themselves better and remain vitalized. It is one of the lovely benefits of learning counseling skills that the methods work just as well for yourself as they do for helping others.

THE AUDIENCE

Counseling Skills for Teachers is intended for two audiences quite similar to one another. It can be used by the population of beginning teachers who are just launching their careers. Many school districts see the need to augment traditional teacher preparation programs with additional training in areas that are often neglected in universities. Among the highest priorities is ensuring that newly hired personnel are equipped with professional and personal survival skills that are likely to increase the new teacher's probability of success. Counseling and consulting skills certainly rate high on the list for beginning teachers, who are trying so hard to earn the trust and respect of their students.

The book can also be used as a primary or secondary text in a variety of education courses that include a component on "helping skills" for teachers. Indeed, many teacher preparation programs include a whole course on the role of educator as counselor/consultant. In other countries, training models exist in which counseling as a specialty in education is unheard of; teachers are expected to function as counselors in addition to their other responsibilities. After all, who spends more time with children and is better positioned to observe them on a daily basis?

OVERVIEW OF CONTENT

This book is derived from a previous volume, *Teacher as Counselor*. We changed the title to *Counseling Skills for Teachers* in 2000, and we also changed some of the content in order to focus more specifically on the skills of helping others rather than the role of functioning in the capacity as a counselor. For this new edition, we have added considerable material on integrating counseling skills and strategies not only in one-to-one problem-solving interactions but also during normal activities in class in which opportunities arise to help students personalize content.

We have also done the following:

1. Expanded the section on assessing and diagnosing problems

2. Included the use of counseling skills in the hallways, playgrounds, and other informal interactions

3. Presented applications of skills to resolving discipline problems and critical incidents that arise in class

4. Mentioned ways that content can be learned from process activities

5. Emphasized making adaptations to cultural differences in using counseling skills

6. Presented cutting-edge brief therapy techniques

7. Discussed how to make effective referrals to other professionals

The first chapter sets the context for what will follow, discussing the variety of roles that teachers play in a school and in students' lives. Whether serving as a coach, club sponsor, playground monitor, mentor, or adult model, you will find opportunities every day, if not each hour, to apply counseling skills in your work.

Chapter 2 helps you look at the big picture of how and why counseling works to help people change their behavior. You will learn about the most important ingredients of any helping strategy, regardless of personal style and theoretical orientation. A number of concise checklists are provided to guide your efforts in applying counseling skills in your work and life.

All teaching and counseling efforts begin with some sort of assessment in which relevant problems are identified and intervention strategies are planned. The basics of diagnosing emotional disorders and student problems are described in Chapter 3 to help sensitize you to the kinds of issues you may encounter.

Chapter 4 forms the heart of the book, describing both the process of counseling relationships and the skills involved in moving students from a stage of confusion to some sort of problem resolution, or at least some degree of understanding. In this chapter, you will learn the basics for creating and maintaining solid helping relationships with students, as well as skills for listening, responding to feelings and content, setting goals, and initiating an action plan.

Chapter 5 applies these skills to classroom or group settings in which you might initiate counseling-related activities as part of your normal curriculum. In addition to including more attention to process in your classroom, you will also learn ways to apply counseling skills to critical incidents and discipline problems that occur frequently.

Chapter 6 examines a crucial but neglected area of most teacher training: how to conduct an effective parent-student conference, using the helping skills previously presented. Practical dimensions of structuring meetings will be described, as well as suggestions for dealing with problems that occur.

Chapter 7 discusses the ways that you can recruit the assistance of other specialists and experts to make your job easier, as well as to ensure that students receive the help they need. It is not enough to merely refer a troubled student for counseling, since most don't follow through with the advice, no matter how well intended. You will learn how to consult with other professionals to coordinate efforts for the good of students.

The concluding chapter describes ways that you can apply the concepts in this book to enrich your own life and improve your own personal functioning. This is useful not only to minimize stress at work but also to vitalize your life.

A NOTE TO READERS

The subjects discussed in this book do not lend themselves to learning by passive means. Although reading chapters about helping skills will enable you to conceptualize how and why various counseling strategies are applied, there is no way that these complex behaviors can become part of your own interpersonal style without considerable practice. This personal integration can take two basic forms:

1. After each idea is presented, ask yourself how you can make it part of your life, how you could use the techniques to enrich your own relationships.

2. Find opportunities to practice new skills in enough situations so that they will become a natural part of your interpersonal style.

At the end of each chapter, we have included a list of suggested reading, should you want to learn more about a particular subject. Of even more importance, we have provided a number of activities that you might complete if you want to apply what you learn to real-life situations. This kind of practice is, of course, one of the most important concepts of effective education: If we expect to influence the way students think, feel, and act, we must develop structures in which they can apply what they learn in multiple situations. This certainly applies to your own attempts to master a set of very difficult skills in a very short period of time.

With sufficient time, energy, and commitment on your part; with a systematic study of helping skills; and with supervised practice in applying them, you can become proficient at integrating counseling and consulting skills as part of your daily teaching roles.

About the Authors

Jeffrey A. Kottler has worked as a teacher and counselor in a variety of settings, including hospitals, mental health centers, schools, clinics, universities, corporations, and private practice. He is currently Professor and Chair of the Department of Counseling at California State University, Fullerton. Jeffrey is the author or coauthor of more than 60 books on education, counseling, and psychology, including *On Being a Teacher: The Human Dimension, Divine Madness: Ten Stories of Creative Struggle, The Client Who Changed Me: Stories of Therapist Personal Transformation, Making Changes Last*, and *Students Who Drive You Crazy: Succeeding With Resistant, Unmotivated, and Otherwise Difficult Young People.*

Ellen Kottler has been a teacher for more than 25 years in public and private schools, universities, alternative schools, and adult education programs. She has worked in inner-city schools as well as suburban and rural settings, and has taught history, mathematics, Spanish, social studies, humanities, and family living. She is currently Lecturer in the Department of Secondary Education at California State University, Fullerton and the Director of the Center for Careers in Teaching. Ellen is the author of *Children With Limited English: Strategies for the Regular Classroom, Secrets to Success for Beginning Elementary School Teachers,* and *Secrets for Secondary School Teachers: How to Succeed in Your First Year.*

Adjusting to Multiple Roles

1

When you reminisce about your own educational experiences and reflect on those teachers who were most inspirational, who made the greatest difference in your life? Who stands out as the teacher you admired most? It's likely that in addition to any expertise or wisdom they demonstrated, there was something about their personal qualities, the ways they carried themselves, their integrity and honesty, that earned your respect and trust. It was not just the knowledge they held that made them such wonderful teachers—it was the personal and passionate way in which they communicated their caring for you. You sensed that they had your best interests in mind. They listened and responded as if you really mattered to them.

Assuming this phenomenon is fairly universal—in other words, that students are influenced not only by instruction but also by a teacher's caring and compassion—then teachers really must have specialized training in all of their various responsibilities; this includes not only your job as a source of knowledge but also your roles as a mentor, caregiver, authority figure, role model, coach, surrogate parent, and limit setter.

A SKILLED HELPER

You have had systematic education in the materials and methods of pedagogy, the construction of lesson plans and completion of individual progress reports, and the use of audiovisual and computer technology. But what about training in the other roles you will play in students' lives—as a model of personal effectiveness, as a compassionate listener, as a skilled helper?

You will be called on daily, if not hourly, to wear a number of different hats and function in a variety of diverse roles for which you may not be adequately prepared. What will you do when a child confides to you that she is pregnant? How will you handle the student who is falling apart emotionally before your eyes? What will you do when you suspect that a child is abusing drugs or is suffering from an eating disorder? What will you say to the child who approaches you for understanding because he feels lonely? What will you do when a student solicits your promise to keep a secret, but then tells you that she is breaking the law and intends to continue doing so?

Teachers are not just receptacles of knowledge who impart pearls of wisdom every time a bell rings. By choosing this profession, you have dedicated yourself to influencing children's lives in a number of different ways. To accomplish this mission, you will do so much more than stand before a classroom of attentive eyes and ears. You will develop relationships with children that are built on trust, mutual respect, and true affection. And from those alliances, children will come to you with their problems. But more often, they will cry out for help in more subtle ways via signs that you will not be able to read without additional training.

Your job is to develop yourself as a skilled helper—a task that will involve mastering a number of counseling and consulting skills. This training will permit you to observe and make sense of what children are thinking, feeling, and doing. It will allow you to gain access to their inner worlds, earn their trust, and truly understand what they are experiencing. From such an empathic position, you will help them feel understood. You will help them reach greater clarity. You will help them make difficult decisions. You will help them take constructive action. When indicated, you will urge them to seek professional help. And they will listen to you because you have the helping skills and an authentic interest in their welfare.

COUNSELING SKILLS FOR TEACHERS

Teachers in other countries function quite differently from the way we do in North America. In parts of Asia, for example, there are no school counselors—not because of lack of funds but rather because of recognition that teachers are the ones who are best positioned to serve in counseling roles. They are the ones, after all, who interact with children on a daily basis. If a child is going to approach an adult for assistance or advice, it will probably not be the person who arranges her schedule once per semester; it will be the teacher whom she has come to trust over many hours of work and play together.

Whether you like it or not, whether you prepare for the role or not, you will be sought out as a confidante by children who have nowhere else to turn. They will expect a number of things from you, some that you cannot deliver (finding the "right" answer), some that you won't have time to do (continue an ongoing counseling type of dialogue), and some that you should not do (take over their lives and tell them what to do). Nevertheless, if you are equipped with some counseling skills, just some basic helping strategies like listening and responding, you will be amazed at the services you can render in helping children gain better clarity of their feelings, better understanding of their motives, and greater resolve in following through on a plan to change their behavior. Adding counseling skills to your repertoire of educational methodologies will help you in a number of ways.

1. You will notice an improvement in your personal relationships. Because learning counseling skills will increase your sensitivity and responsiveness, this training will affect the ways you relate to other people. You will notice yourself becoming more attuned to others' feelings. You will become clearer in your communications and more expressive of your own needs. Finally, you will experience a renewed commitment to working toward greater intimacy in your relationships with friends and family.

I've been amazed at how attentive I am to my family when I get home. At first, I was pretty resistant to learning this stuff. Gee, the last thing in the world I need is more work to do; I'm already so overwhelmed with stuff. But I've been delighted at how learning to be more responsive to my students at school has also made me a better listener to other people in my life.

2. You will become more respected as a colleague in your school. Just as high-level interpersonal skills allow you to create better relationships in your personal life, they give you the confidence and ability to forge constructive alliances with administrators, other teachers in your school, and support staff. Everyone wants a friend who listens well, is empathic, is a clear thinker, and responds to his or her needs. One other benefit: When you learn to speak the language of counselors, you will be able to make more appropriate referrals of children in need of help.

I have one friend who's a counselor in the district, and he was telling me how he gets about 90 percent of his referrals from about 10 percent of the teachers. I'm one of them, I guess, who refers lots of kids. I don't think this means that my students are more screwed up than others, just that I pay attention to their emotional stuff. I know I can't help them myself, but I try to get them started and then have the counselor close the deal.

3. You will become more influential in your work in the classroom. Children respond best to teachers who model what they themselves would like to become someday. They respect you and respond to you not only for your expertise but also for your caring and compassion. Quite simply, counseling skills will allow you to create better relationships with children in a shorter period of time. Students will be more inclined to trust you and to work hard to gain your respect if they sense the same from you. These skills thus form the glue bonding together everything else you have learned about being a superlative teacher.

Kids see me at their plays, softball and soccer games, and recitals. They know that I care about them not because I tell them I do but because I show them by my behavior. I'm someone, maybe the only person in their lives, whom they can truly count on.

4. You will be able to address children's most important concerns at the same time you counteract your own fears of ineptitude and failure. Beginning teachers, in particular, have myriad apprehensions regarding their own abilities and potential as professionals. Several teacher education students, on the verge of beginning their student teaching, talk about some of their greatest fears.

Karyn feels quite confident about her ability to relate to children; however, she feels most unprepared conducting parent conferences: *"I dread having to explain to parents why I do things the way I do. I don't know how on earth I will ever get them to try different things at home that will make my job easier."*

Randi, as well, worries most about how she will react to certain parents—especially the ones who don't seem to care about their children: *"I'm afraid I will lose my temper, become completely out of control, when I talk to some of these parents who do such damage to their kids. I know if I do that I will just end up hurting the kids as well as my own situation."*

Travis mentions that his greatest fear is encountering the child who is being neglected or abused at home: *"I know what I am supposed to do: report the situation to protective services. But sometimes things aren't so clear. What happens to the child after I do that? Maybe I'll just make things worse. I just hope I have the courage to do what is right."*

Tanya is quite nervous about her responsibility of being a model for kids: *"It's so scary to think that everything I do and say will be watched so closely. Children are so impressionable, and I certainly would like to be the kind of person whom they admire. That is going to be hard for me because I'm not used to that kind of responsibility. I was the youngest in my family, and I'm used to looking up to everyone else."*

Nick wonders if he will ever learn to disconnect from the intense emotional problems that he will encounter as a special education teacher: *"Will I be able to save enough of myself for my family when I get home? Some of these kids are just so messed up and so needy—they just need so much attention. If I am going to last very long, I know I will have to back off, to separate their problems from my own."*

Cassie is reluctantly honest in admitting she has a problem with patience: *"It boggles my mind to think that I will be in a room with 20 kindergarteners for six hours every day. Will I have the restraint to be gentle when some of the little ones try to push me over the edge?"* She also wonders if she will be able to keep her biases under wraps: *"I know we are all prejudiced to some extent. I just hope that I can withhold my judgments when I'm dealing with a troubled student. Such a volatile situation could have disastrous results if I'm not able to keep my own opinions to myself."*

Nila considers herself oversensitive to criticism and overly cautious about everything she says. She wonders how that will affect her ability to be helpful: *"I become obsessed with saying the 'right' thing the 'right' way. I don't want to hurt or embarrass anyone. I'm concerned that I won't do anything at all because I don't want to make any mistakes."*

Each of these examples illustrates another way that counseling skills will help you neutralize your own fears of failure in trying to be helpful to children. That is the wonder and power of this training: As you become more skilled and accomplished as a helper of others, you become more proficient at applying what you know to your own life.

Counseling skills will help you not only adjust more flexibly to the variety of roles you will take on in your classroom and school, but also help yourself in a number of ways to which we already alluded:

- Enhancing the intimacy of all your relationships
- Making you more sensitive to your own inner feelings, as well as more fluent in expressing them
- Working through interpersonal conflicts more easily
- Handling discipline problems with less disruption and drama
- Talking yourself through upsetting situations in order to reduce negative feelings
- Processing unforeseen problems in constructive, systematic ways
- Confronting your own unresolved issues that get in the way of your being more effective personally and professionally

What all this means is that the more proficient you become in the counseling skills presented in this book, the more attractive you become as a person as well as a teacher.

LIFE INSIDE THE CLASSROOM

Teaching is, first and foremost, a helping profession. While structuring a learning environment, the educator has to be aware of students' physical, emotional, and social needs, as well as their intellectual needs. Teachers must create a pleasant atmosphere in their classrooms where students will be safe physically and secure psychologically to explore the world of ideas. From the moment the students enter the room, the teacher begins to develop rapport with them and build trust—whether they stay for 45 minutes or the whole day. The educator must be kind and helpful, inviting and stimulating, as students are guided through learning activities. The teacher must work toward building the self-respect and self-esteem of each student. Furthermore, he or she must work toward fostering tolerance and cooperation in the classroom by adapting methods and styles according to the cultural backgrounds and individual needs of students. The teacher must prepare the children to interact with one another in a positive, constructive manner. Students must learn to be good citizens, to interpret the events taking place around them, and to make decisions. It is the teacher's responsibility to provide these experiences.

In addition to these roles, the educator must get to know each student, his or her ups and downs, and the momentary and long-term stresses of each individual. The teacher must offer support and encouragement to each child—from Fernando, who lost a portion of his finger in an accident; to Amy, whose new baby brother came home the night before; to Vanessa, who has such a low frustration tolerance; to Brian, whose father moved out of the house last week. Changing friendships, fear of failure, and other issues occupy the minds of students. And the teacher must decide how best to approach the events that take place in the lives of children—one-to-one, through reading a story, or through group discussion.

At the same time, the teacher must pay attention to external events that disrupt the daily schedule. Change interrupts the learning process, whether it is an impromptu pep assembly, a fire drill, or academic testing. A crisis in the community will take precedence over any planned topic. In several cities, for example, acts of violence have distracted kids from concentrating on relatively less important priorities, such as homework. Children needed to be reassured that they were safe and that nothing would harm them. They talked about the impact of violence; for example, in one city, they talked about how far they had to go to get food stamps after the welfare office had been burned. Immediate needs had to be addressed. Similarly, students in another town talked about depression, loneliness, and the responsibilities of friendship after one student tried to commit suicide.

Much of the learning that takes place in class has little to do with the scheduled lesson plans. Kids have their own agendas and their own interests, many of which have little to do with whatever you think is important. After all, how important can history, handwriting, or math be if your major priority in life is finding enough food to eat, making up with your best friend, getting a part in a play, or stopping others from teasing you?

Life inside the classroom involves not only the scheduled activities and subjects you have planned, but also many other issues that will arise spontaneously from current events or students' lives. You must be ready to address these important issues rather than ignore them. Even more challenging, you must find ways to integrate what you teach into the cultural and personal context of each student. Counseling skills can help you draw out students better to find out what they know and desire, as well as to respond to these needs more powerfully.

A DAY IN THE LIFE

A teacher will interact with counselors, social workers, school psychologists, deans, principals, parents, and other teachers—not to mention hundreds of children—on a regular basis. Whether evaluating the present or planning for the future, discussing a new policy or the behavior of an individual student, the teacher will be called on to give his or her views and recommendations. To work cooperatively with other professionals and parents, the teacher must also be able to establish rapport with these adults.

Relationships with students and other professionals are always evolving. Our goal is to provide you with the inspiration and motivation to develop the interpersonal skills so vital for the effective teacher. You will develop a clearer idea of what most teachers face if you watch over the shoulder of one professional who goes about fulfilling her daily multiple roles as a teacher.

As Mrs. Neubrith opens the door to her car and prepares to gather her things to start her day, she sees a group of kids congregating by the side of the building. Her heart skips a beat: Will she have to break up a fight? Perhaps they are transacting some illicit business or improper behavior that she will have to stop. No, this time she discovers an innocent gathering of friends who are huddled together for protection against the cold. She breathes a sigh of relief.

It is 7:10 in the morning, and already Mrs. Neubrith, high school teacher extraordinaire, is beginning the first of several hundred interactions she will have throughout the day with different children and colleagues. As she approaches the door and mentally reviews what lies ahead, besides her usual teaching responsibilities, she knows that she will talk to one of the assistant principals about a new student in her class. She needs to get in to see the principal about a workshop she would like to attend that will require supplemental funding. One of her lunch partners is going through a divorce, so she knows that will be a focus of discussion during the day. Also, she was alerted that someone from the district office would be monitoring some of her classes for a research study he is conducting.

During her preparation period, Mrs. Neubrith will talk to the school counselor about one of her students who is tracked in college prep but has much more interest in going into the military. As the day continues, a student who flunked her driver's test will literally cry on her shoulder. She will catch a student cheating in her fourth-hour class, a situation that will involve speaking to the other assistant principal; the student twice;

and the student's parents, who will adamantly refuse to acknowledge that their darling son could have committed such an immoral act. Another student will approach her with excitement at having recently become engaged; this student feels a special affinity for Mrs. Neubrith because she and her fiancé first met in Mrs. Neubrith's class.

An assortment of other interactions will take place with the school secretary, several colleagues who are organizing support groups for children of divorce, and literally hundreds of children who pass her in the halls. She can see their pleading eyes, their distraught expressions, the disappointment in their faces, their raging hormones, their volatile emotions, their passion and excitement, and she feels overwhelmed by all the pain and neediness she can sense. Mrs. Neubrith tries to acknowledge each person and realizes that they all want so much more from her than she can possibly deliver.

As you follow Mrs. Neubrith through an all-too-typical day, you notice the great number of people with whom she comes into contact and the variety of situations in which she uses her interpersonal skills. One moment she is talking to a student who is apprehensive about a family relocation; she moves on to talk to a boy who feels like a failure because he was cut from the basketball team; then, she speaks to a student who is returning from drug rehabilitation; next, she is advising a student about college plans. A great portion of her day is spent interacting with others as people turn to her for guidance and as she lets others know she cares about what is happening to them.

Then, there are all the things that come up during her class discussions. In one class, there is a heated argument between two students about affirmative action that quickly takes on racist overtones. In another class, one minute they are following the scheduled lesson, and the next moment someone asks a question about the upcoming exam that somehow deteriorates into a gripe session about how unfair the world is. In another class, a foolproof activity that normally is quite exciting turns out to be incredibly boring, and she can't figure out why or what she can do to change directions.

Although this day in the life of a teacher involves the experience of a high school teacher, the same pattern unfolds for those in elementary education. Every hour presents a different challenge, another test of your concentration, sensitivity, and interpersonal skills. In each case, you are required to remain calm and in control, to sort out what is going on, and then to select the appropriate response from the hundreds of possibilities you can think of at the time.

Whether you like it or not, whether you are prepared or not, students will seek you out for help in making decisions about everything from accepting a party invitation to what classes they should take. They ask for help in sorting out values and evaluating the ethics of the situations they face. They come to share the events that take place in their lives: a new dog, frustration over a poor grade, rejected friendship, a death in the family. They turn to you with questions of manners and etiquette.

The ways you respond to these situations, the fluency and ease with which you adjust to multiple roles, will influence greatly the quality of the educational experiences you provide. Your knowledge of counseling skills will affect your relationships with the children with whom you work, your friendships and affiliations with colleagues, and even the quality of your relationships with the people you love the most.

SUGGESTED ACTIVITIES

1. About which aspects of teaching are you most apprehensive? For which roles do you feel most unprepared? After reflecting on these questions, (a) write down your responses and put the pages in a safe place where you can reread what you wrote several years from now, and (b) share your reactions in a group of peers meeting to discuss their fears.

2. Interview a cross-section of children representing different grade levels to find out the roles they would like to see teachers play in their lives. Encourage them to be as specific as possible in describing what teachers could do to be helpful to them.

3. Shadow a teacher for a day and note the variety of roles he or she plays with an assortment of different people. Organize your observations of the teacher's behavior into some broad categories of roles that were played—as lecturer, problem solver, secretary, or whatever.

SUGGESTED READING

Corey, M. S., & Corey, G. (2007). *Becoming a helper* (5th ed.). Pacific Grove, CA: Brooks/Cole.

Glasgow, N. A. (2006). *What successful teachers do in diverse classrooms.* Thousand Oaks, CA: Corwin Press.

Hazler, R. J. (1998). *Helping in the hallways: Advanced strategies for enhancing school relationships.* Thousand Oaks, CA: Corwin Press.

Kottler, J. A. (2003). *On being a therapist.* San Francisco: Jossey-Bass.

Kottler, J. A., Zehm, S. J., & Kottler, E. (2005). *On being a teacher: The human dimension* (3rd ed.). Thousand Oaks, CA: Corwin Press.

Palmer, P. J. (1998). *The courage to teach: Exploring the inner landscape of a teacher's life.* San Francisco: Jossey-Bass.

Understanding the   **2**
Process of Helping

I t isn't your job to do counseling on a regular basis or to act as a ready confidante for all your students. You will not have the time, opportunity, or training to serve in those roles; even if you did, you won't have the energy. Nevertheless, there will be daily instances in which children will reach out to you for understanding, if not for guidance.

SOME SUGGESTIONS FOR
LEARNING COUNSELING SKILLS

Some rudimentary background in several skills will allow you to help them more effectively. First, some basic ideas to keep in mind:

1. *You cannot learn helping skills by reading about them.* If you are serious about augmenting your repertoire of interpersonal skills, you must practice them.

2. *Being in a helping role is not natural.* In spite of what you may have heard, employing counseling skills means doing a number of things that are unnatural, such as being nonjudgmental and putting your own needs aside.

3. *You are dealing with concerns, not problems.* Problems imply that there are solutions, even right ones; yet most often, personal issues have no single answer. Most of us continue to struggle with the same issues our whole lives.

4. *Don't give advice.* By telling people what you think they should do with their lives, one of two things can happen, both of which can lead to negative consequences. First, if you think you know what is best for someone and you tell him or her what to do, the results could turn out disastrous—*you* will be blamed for the rest of your life for being the one at

fault. The only thing worse than giving bad advice is giving good advice. If what you tell someone to do works out beautifully, then what this person has learned is that when he or she doesn't know what to do in the future, he or she should consult someone else. After all, you have reinforced the idea that the person is incapable of making decisions on his or her own.

5. *Don't try to do too much.* The most frequent difficulty that beginning helpers have is, ironically, trying to do too much. Remember, it is the child's issue—all you can do is help students not feel so alone, show that you understand, and demonstrate that you support them.

6. *Before you begin, slip into a "helping" mode.* Similar to meditation and other altered states of consciousness, helping another person involves focused concentration. When you decide to help someone, you are making a temporary decision to clear your mind of all your own stuff, to resist distractions, and to stay nonjudgmental about what you are hearing. Furthermore, except when children are in danger of hurting themselves or someone else, you are committed to keeping private communications confidential.

7. *Don't let yourself feel overwhelmed.* We will present a brief overview of material that would require three years of full-time study in order to develop competency. It is neither realistic nor reasonable for you to expect to put to use all the ideas and skills presented. Our goal is merely to help you expand your current levels of interpersonal effectiveness. As you evolve in your career, you will find many opportunities for inservice training, workshops, graduate courses, CDs and DVDs, and books that will help you become progressively more proficient in these skills.

8. *Be patient with yourself.* Although much of this material may sound familiar to you, there is a distinctly different and unique posture that counselors take when they are in helping roles. This is not at all a natural state of being since you must put your own needs aside and focus totally and completely on the other person's experience. As with any new skills, some of them will feel awkward and clumsy. Be realistic with yourself as to what you can reasonably expect from a first introduction to new material. This is not to say that you can't experience major transformations in the ways you deal with people in your life—simply realize that this will take work, practice, and patience.

HELPING ATTITUDES

Although we are about to present you with the process and skills of helping, it is important to keep in mind that counseling relationships involve a lot more than mastery of expert techniques. There is a helping attitude that counselors adopt when in session—a state of mind that keeps them clear, focused, and receptive. This is a different state of consciousness than would normally be practiced, one that is not unlike a meditative state in which all attention, energy, and mindfulness is focused on a single activity; that is, helping another person to find peace.

We mentioned being nonjudgmental as one facet of a helping posture. Other features that have been demonstrated again and again as crucial to developing solid relationships are authenticity, genuineness, caring, respect, and compassion. These are not just words to which we give lip service; these attitudes are the essence of what it means to make contact with and truly understand another human being.

Practice a Helping Mind-Set

Learning helping attitudes takes practice. In fact, normally we spend well over a month drilling counseling students in the process by which they can get into a helping mind-set, one that allows for greater awareness of the other, as well as more focused concentration. These are the steps involved, and we suggest you try them out in a conversation with someone.

- *Take a deep breath.* As in yoga, this is called a *cleansing breath.* Gently push aside all distractions, all competing thoughts, and focus completely on this other person.
- *Focus your attention.* Each time your attention wanders, or you can feel some intrusive thought, just gently push it aside. Bring the focus back to the other person, giving him or her your full attention. This is *exactly* like a meditative state in which you are practicing mindfulness.
- *Stop yourself from making judgments.* Stay as neutral and accepting as you can. Even if you don't approve of the person's behavior, you can still accept him or her *as a person.* If a student senses your slightest disapproval or criticism, any chance you had to be helpful may be lost.
- *Access your compassion and empathy.* As you look at this person, open your heart in such a way that you actually feel and communicate your deep concern and caring.

If you watch a professional tennis player prior to serving the ball, a pitcher in baseball, or any other expert in human performance, you will notice they follow a ritual designed to help them enter a zone of maximum concentration. You will see them take a deep breath, as well as follow a prescribed series of movements or gestures, all of which help them concentrate only on the thing that they are doing. It is the same with practicing counseling skills: you enter into a zone in which you convey, and feel, greater compassion; in which you can hear and see things that might otherwise remain invisible; and in which you can give more of yourself than would otherwise be possible.

Unlike the skills we present throughout this book, you cannot learn these attitudes merely by practicing them. In order to feel caring and compassionate toward children (or anyone), especially when they are going out of their way to be unlovable, you must make a major commitment. Your dedication is obvious because you have already chosen the profession of teaching.

Remember, though, that the act of helping is not just an applied set of skills and techniques; it also represents your attempt to bring comfort and constructive input to someone who is struggling or in great pain.

AN INTEGRATIVE APPROACH TO COUNSELING

You are well aware that educators have long debated the best way to promote learning. You have studied dozens of theories, each of which presents an apparently unique explanation to account for how children learn. You have also been exposed to considerable difference of opinion as to the single best way that teachers should operate. You have heard that teachers should concentrate primarily on trying to reinforce and behaviorally manage children's behavior. You have also heard that a developmental, constructivist, humanistic, or cognitive approach works equally well. The really confusing thing, however, is that *all* of your professors and the authors you've read seem to be right: There are, indeed, a number of conflicting theories of teaching that are all effective even though they rely on supposedly different, even contradictory, principles.

These debates are no less strident in the counseling field. There are as many as 400 different systems of helping that claim to have evidence indicating that their way of working is the best—that they have discovered "truth." Rather than concentrating on the unique features of different approaches, we focus on the elements that almost all practitioners would agree are important. Any generic helping approach, whether practiced by counselors, psychologists, psychiatrists, social workers, teachers, or witch doctors—whether in our culture or elsewhere—will have similar operative ingredients.

Altered States of Consciousness

The object of all helping approaches, whether in teaching or counseling, is to initiate perceptual changes and to influence thinking, feeling, and behavior. Efforts to accomplish these tasks are more likely to be successful if the student is in a receptive mode. This increased receptivity to influence takes place when a person is in a more suggestible mood, a state that can be created by anyone who constructs a helping environment that is conducive to change. There are things you can do to increase your status, expertise, and power in children's eyes and thereby help them to be more receptive to what you have to offer.

Increasing Altered States

- Capture student attention and interest through introducing novel stimuli.
- Vary your voice and body language to increase or decrease arousal as needed.
- Use relaxation methods to help students remain calm.
- Increase credibility by demonstrating expertise in areas of student interest.
- Make predictions about what will happen, and then allow students to confirm your predictions.
- Use music and other special effects to put students in a receptive mood.
- Increase student receptivity by decreasing perceived threats.

Placebo Effects

A universal aspect of any change process involves influencing children's belief systems in such a way that they become convinced that the procedure will be successful. Doctors do this when they offer relatively benign medications with the accompaniment, "I know this will make you feel better." We do essentially the same thing when we are able to communicate to children that what we do works very well. By believing in our own power to be helpful, we offer hope and inspiration to people who have often given up:

I'm so glad you decided to come and speak with me. I have heard a number of children express similar concerns to those that you have mentioned. I have no doubt that you will feel much better after we talk, and I just know that I can help you.

This message has an almost hypnotic quality, communicating our belief that the process we offer does, indeed, work. Compare it to another introductory statement that is filled with doubt:

Well, uh, that is really a tough situation you're in. I really don't have much experience talking about this sort of thing. I'm not sure there's anything I can do. What the heck, we might as well talk a little and maybe something useful can happen—but I doubt it.

This latter statement might sound like a humorous exaggeration but you'd be amazed at the ineffective, clumsy ways that teachers try to be helpful but do so in a way that they communicate nothing but discouraging, pessimistic outcomes. While you don't want to distort your level of expertise and training, you do want to give people hope.

Therapeutic Relationship

Of all the universal features that we will mention, the helping relationship may be the most powerful factor of all. Most people strive for intimacy in their lives; each person wishes to be connected to and understood by others. Long ago, we all belonged to close-knit tribes of friends, relatives, and neighbors who were all concerned with one another; however, modern life offers a more fragmented, disconnected existence. Children hunger for close relationships, as do adults. One of the common elements of every helping system is an emphasis on creating an alliance that is open, trusting, accepting, and safe. This helping relationship becomes intrinsically healing in some ways. It offers comfort and support. It motivates risk taking. It becomes the core for everything else we do in the helping process.

Although you may be overly concerned with conducting a helping encounter in the "right" way, or practicing counseling skills appropriately, the bottom line is that it will be your relationship with students that makes the most difference. If students feel your sincerity, your trust, your commitment to them, even your love, they will often feel nourished and supported in ways that can make a huge difference in their lives.

Building a Relationship

- Start with small, incremental steps.
- Be sensitive to the student's readiness level.
- Pay close attention to what draws the person closer, or pushes the person away.
- Communicate your caring and intense interest.
- Show your warmth and accessibility.
- Prove you heard and understood what was said.
- Demonstrate your commitment to the student.
- Be consistent.
- Model openness and honesty.
- Practice deep compassion and empathy.

Cathartic Process

Sigmund Freud discovered long ago that when people are given the opportunity to explore what is bothering them, to talk without interruption about their fears and concerns, they often feel much better afterward. Every counseling approach has cathartic processes built into it in which the person is permitted and encouraged to talk about whatever is most troublesome. By developing just a few relationship-building skills, you will be able to capitalize on these last two elements exceedingly well.

Essentially, much of what happens in counseling sessions is that a safe place is created for people to tell their stories. We are not talking about the *rehearsed* stories that are retold over and over as if recited from rote memory. Rather, we are talking about the opportunity to speak honestly and deeply about life experiences in such a way that one feels heard and understood. Everyone has secrets. Everyone feels shame about something in his or her life. Everyone struggles with things in the past that may have been traumatic or terrifying. And most people feel significantly better if they can talk to someone else about what they have lived through, or what they are going through now.

Consciousness Raising

Any significant change means alterations in the way you look at yourself, at others, and at the world. As teachers, you are particularly well suited to promote these kinds of changes. You are interested in not only increasing children's awareness of the world but also of themselves in relation to others. This element of counseling is thus concerned with promoting more self-understanding and self-discovery—tasks that are certainly within the province of a teacher's role.

We are speaking here about helping students gain a better understanding of themselves, and of the world. Depending on the situation, the student, and your approach, this could take one of many forms:

- Highlighting discrepancies: *"Interesting that you are having trouble in my class when you did so well in math. What do you suppose is the difference?"*
- Connecting patterns: *"This is the third time that you have had trouble in this same area. There seems to be a pattern developing."*
- Confronting nondefensively: *"You say that you are a loser but I notice that you have several friends who seem to care very much for you."*
- Encouraging constructive risk taking: *"What can you do to gain more confidence in this area so you don't have to experience such fear in the future?"*
- Challenging exaggerations: *"You describe yourself as* always *pleasing others, no matter what. But I've noticed several times that you have disagreed with me."*

- Asking difficult questions without providing answers: *"What do you think that means that so many of your friends are doing that?"*
- Modeling uncertainty: *"I'm not sure myself what is going on sometimes. I have been struggling with making sense of that my whole life."*

In all of these, and other forms, you are challenging students to look more deeply at ways they characteristically function. You are helping them to make sense of their own behavior. While such insights are usually not sufficient to promote lasting change by themselves, they still promote the kind of self-reflective activity that encourages becoming more thoughtful and intentional.

Reinforcement

Counseling uses the therapeutic relationship as a means to systematically shape more fully functioning behavior and to extinguish self-defeating actions. When the child reports that for the first time she really understands why she has been having certain problems, we offer immediate support; likewise, when she engages in previous maladaptive behavior, we deliberately ignore or discourage those responses. During conversations this reinforcement may be quite subtle: As the child speaks of feeling powerful and in control, we smile and nod, whereas when she acts passive and dependent, we appear more neutral and less supportive of this behavior. Of course, the challenge in applying any behavioral principle is to make clear that although we approve and disapprove of certain behavior, we always continue to care unconditionally for the child.

Rehearsal

Helping encounters provide particularly good opportunities for children to practice new behaviors within the safety of the therapeutic relationship and with plenty of feedback. For example, a child dreads telling his parents that he wants to join the Debate Club instead of trying out for football (a sport he despises) because he thinks they will make fun of him. The teacher helps him rehearse a conversation that he will initiate later that day when his father comes home from work:

Teacher: *"Okay, so pretend that I am your dad. Tell me what you want to say."*

Child: *"I don't think I can do this. He just won't listen."*

Teacher: *"Are you saying that you don't even want to try?"*

Child: *"Well, I guess so."*

Teacher: *"You don't sound very convincing."*

Child: *"Yes! Yes, I do want to try talking to him."*

Teacher: (Slipping into the role of father) *"So, Son, what did you want to talk to me about?"*

Child: *"Um, Dad, I, ah, I just wanted to . . . I mean . . . Oh, never mind."*

Teacher: (Offering support) *"Well, that was a start anyway. This time, just say what you want to say. Don't worry about how he will respond."*

As this coached dialogue continues, the boy is helped to articulate what is most important for him to communicate. He receives feedback on strategies that he might try. Most important, he has the opportunity to practice acting in more powerful ways, an experience that will serve him well in life even if the confrontation with his father does not work out as he would prefer.

Task Facilitation

One of the most important things we can ever do for children is encourage them to try new ways of behaving. Most approaches to counseling include helping people complete therapeutic tasks. Obviously, the child in the previous example has a tremendous amount of reluctance to speak with his father. If we can define a successful outcome as not so much getting one's way as trying to act courageously, then the child will feel better about himself no matter how his father responds to his overture.

Many counseling sessions end with the client being asked the critical question: "So, given what we talked about today, what are you going to *do* this week?"

The emphasis is on "doing" because talking is often not enough to promote lasting change. In helping conversations, as in other aspects of life, people can have perfect understanding of what they are doing, why and how it is self-destructive, and yet still continue with the behavior anyway. Regardless of how the sessions are structured, it is often useful to ask students what they intend to do that will get them closer to their desired goals.

Each preceding element just reviewed is part of most counseling efforts, regardless of the theoretical persuasion of the practitioner. As we look in greater depth at exactly what is involved in a counseling encounter with a child, keep in mind that this is a generic approach, one that most professionals would agree is somewhat universal. As you come to gain more experience and training, you may very well adapt this general approach to one that fits better with your personality, teaching style, and student population.

A REVIEW OF THE COUNSELING PROCESS

The counseling process follows a series of logical and sequential stages, not unlike what you might invent intuitively from any problem-solving effort. Although these components are presented as if they were discrete parts, in fact the boundaries often overlap to the point where it's hard to determine at which stage you are. The important point is to have an overview of how helping takes place, the stages that children usually go through, and a blueprint for where you are headed once you identify your current position in the process.

In addition, several different counseling approaches are linked with particular stages in the process. Although each of the skills that will be reviewed might be employed at any time, typically they are used more during particular times. For example, it makes sense to ask questions more often during the exploration stage and initiate goal setting more often during the action stage.

Assessment

Before you can attempt any effort at being helpful, you have to have some idea as to what is going on. Counselors and therapists call this the identification of the presenting complaint, but it is simply a systematic effort to help the child describe what is bothersome. It is also crucial to collect any important background information relevant to the child's concerns.

A student tells you he is depressed and asks you what to do about that. Before you could even begin to address this problem, there are many things that would first need to be sorted out. Among the initial questions you might have are: What do you mean by "depressed?" There are so many possible interpretations of this self-description. Are we dealing with the kind of chronic, intractable depression that leads to thoughts of suicide, or rather just feeling disappointed over something?

As you imagine yourself conducting an assessment, it may occur to you that there are a number of skills you will need that are probably not already part of your professional repertoire. The next chapter reviews in greater detail the particular skills required, but for now, we will simply indicate which skills are important in the various stages. To begin, the counseling skills most often associated with an assessment are these:

1. Asking questions that explore the nature of the problem, gather relevant information, and prompt the student to continue describing experiences

2. Reflecting the child's thoughts and feelings to encourage deeper level exploration and communicate your understanding of what is being said

3. Clarifying the content of what is being presented in such a way that both you and the student reach agreement on the main themes

As an example of this process in action, imagine that a child tells you he is upset because he doesn't have many friends. What would you want to know before you could help this child? Here are a few inquiries that might be considered:

- What do you mean, you don't have many friends?
- Who *are* you close to?
- What have you tried to do so far to resolve this difficulty?
- When you are feeling down, what do you do about it?
- Who knows about this concern of yours?
- What do you hope I can do to help you?

By using reflective skills that encourage the child to elaborate on what he has presented, you will find that these questions rarely need to be asked directly. Eventually, both you and the child will have a clearer idea of what the child is struggling with, and with which part of the problem he most wants assistance.

Exploration

Once you have identified the presenting complaints, the next logical step is to dig deeper into what is going on to discover how this concern is related to other aspects of the child's life. You will continue to use reflective skills to help him clarify what he is feeling and thinking. Applying the skill of *advanced-level empathy* will help him get at the hidden, disguised, and subtle nuances of his experience. Empathy means that you are able to get inside someone else's skin to the point that you can sense what he or she is going through. In this exploration stage, you will use your sensitivity and understanding of the child's experience to help him move to deeper levels of awareness.

A boy without friends might be helped to explore the depth of his feelings of loneliness and estrangement from others. He would become aware of how much he misses having close friends and how much he wishes he could change his situation. With probing from his teacher, he also articulates some of the anger he feels toward his parents for moving him away from his old neighborhood, where he had been perfectly content. Prior to this conversation, he had never been able to say out loud how much he still grieved the loss of his old friends and how resentful he still felt for being pulled away without his consent.

Understanding

The deeper the exploration of one's feelings and thoughts, the more profound the insights that are generated as a result of this process. The helper, at this point, uses more active skills such as confrontation, interpretation, self-disclosure, and the giving of information to help the child understand his own role in creating his difficulty. Furthermore, insights are typically generated around understanding why and how the problem developed, what the child is doing to sabotage improvement, and what themes are being repeated over and over in his life.

Types of Insight That Can Be Generated

- Becoming aware of deep feelings. *"I didn't know I felt so angry about that."*
- Grasping unconscious desires. *"When I got upset with you, I guess I was really mad at my mom for grounding me."*
- Learning to be vigilant about certain behavior. *"I didn't realize that I raise my voice at the end of my sentences, turning everything into a question."*
- Owning denied parts of self. *"I'm not always such a goody-goody person, I guess. Sometimes I can be mischievous, trying to stir things up for their entertainment value."*
- Understanding hidden payoffs to self-defeating behavior. *"I never really thought that there were any advantages to staying depressed. But now that I think about it, I guess I do get a lot of sympathy. Nobody expects much of me. And I have a license to be irritable whenever I want."*
- Confronting irrational thinking that gets in the way. *"Okay, so it isn't actually terrible that I got cut from the team. But you gotta' admit, it's a little disappointing after I worked so hard."*
- Constructing an alternative view of personal reality. *"It's not so much that I'm a failure as I sometimes don't end up finishing what I start."*

The lonely child is confronted with the realization that his prior life was not as wonderful as he makes it out to be. In fact, he was also lonely in his old neighborhood; the only reason it seemed as if he had more friends was because there were more children around the immediate vicinity of his home. He still had not been close to many others. Therefore, he began to accept more responsibility for his own plight. He looked at his fears of being rejected and his strategies of scaring other people away before they had the chance to reject him. He also learned about the self-defeating ways in which he stopped himself from initiating more relationships: He told himself negative things and exaggerated the consequences of what could go wrong if somebody did not want to play with him. Finally, his teacher helped him understand that he did have the power to change this whole pattern of his life if only he were willing to take some risks and try some new ways of acting.

Action

Although understanding and insight are wonderful things, without action to change one's behavior, they lack affective power. There are many people walking around this earth who understand, with perfect clarity, why they are so messed up, but they refuse to do anything to change their ways. The action stage of helping is thus geared to helping children translate what they know and understand into a plan that will get them what they want.

The first part of this action process involves having the child establish goals that he or she wishes to reach. Next, using a variety of skills ranging from problem solving to role-playing, the teacher helps the child generate a list of viable alternative courses of action, narrow them down to those that seem most realistic and attractive, and then make a commitment to follow through on declared intentions.

The lonely boy is helped to clarify exactly what he would like to be able to do that he is unable or unwilling to do—most notably, (a) initiate new relationships, (b) overcome his fears of rejection, and (c) stop doing things that tend to drive people away. He is helped to define more specifically what these goals mean; in other words, to break down into smaller steps what it means to initiate relationships or what specific things he is prone to doing that turn people off. He is then helped to digest small, bite-size pieces of his ultimate goal, slowly making incremental progress. He might start out by initiating a pleasant exchange with someone in his class or sharing his dessert during lunch. From there, he might eventually work up to asking someone new if he could join him or her for lunch. After practicing these realistic tasks that he would assign himself, he would be able to invite someone over to his house to play and, more important, not be devastated if he or she could not or would not come.

Evaluation

The final stage in the helping process involves evaluating with the child the extent to which he or she has reached desired goals. This systematic assessment of progress helps you measure the impact of your interventions and helps the child take inventory of what has been accomplished as well as what is left to do.

Because there are limits to the time and opportunities that you have as a teacher to guide a child all the way through this process, referral will play an important part of your helping effort. If you can do nothing else, you want children to have had a good experience talking to you so that they will be more inclined to take your direction when you urge them to seek additional help.

One struggling student, for example, did make considerable progress in overcoming her reluctance to reach out to others. More important, the teacher helped her to clarify her feelings about her plight and accept responsibility that it was something that she was doing to herself rather than something that was being done to her.

In addition to her social shyness, this girl also had some other difficulties, such as a low frustration tolerance, a nonsupportive home life, and a history of giving up when things didn't go her way. Because of these complications, progress became erratic, although certainly noticeable. The teacher realized that she had neither the time nor the inclination to work on a deeper level with the child. He therefore decided, in his evaluative process with her, that she needed more help than he could offer. He addressed her reluctance to start over with someone else and reassured her that he would still be available in a supportive capacity. The child was then receptive to accepting the suggestion that she consult with the school counselor and work out with him whether that setting, or one in the community, would be the best place for her to continue working on herself.

The Helping Process

Stage	Skills
Assessment	Attending
	Listening
	Focusing
	Observing
Exploration	Reflecting feelings
	Responding to content
	Probing, questioning
	Feeling/empathy
Understanding	Interpreting
	Confronting
	Challenging
	Information giving
	Self-disclosing
Action	Goal setting
	Role-playing
	Reinforcing
	Decision making
Evaluation	Questioning
	Summarizing
	Supporting

THE LINK BETWEEN THE COUNSELING PROCESS AND HELPING SKILLS

Now that you have an understanding of the big picture of functioning in a counseling role with a child, you can appreciate that you will need a number of skills to capitalize on therapeutic elements and to move through the sequential stages of helping. In some cases, you can actually complete all the stages to a satisfactory resolution of the issues, sometimes in a single brief conversation. Most of the time, however, it will be more realistic to concentrate on exploring the issues a bit and leaving it to another time, or another professional, to work things through fully. Your main job is simply to show students that you are a concerned and skilled listener, that you can demonstrate your understanding of their experience, and that you are someone on whom they can count.

SUGGESTED ACTIVITIES

1. Define how a professional helping relationship is different from a relationship with friends.

2. Think of an unresolved issue in your life. Apply the steps of the counseling process to work yourself through (a) an assessment of the issue, (b) an understanding of the underlying themes and connected issues, (c) an action plan of what you propose to do, and (d) how you intend to evaluate the results of your effort.

3. Being nonjudgmental and accepting are important elements in the helping process. Identify several subjects that may come up in conversations with children and about which you feel very strongly (abortion, drug use, sexual activity, discrimination, and so on). Imagine that a child expresses values that are the antithesis of your own. Formulate responses that would avoid imposing a critical, judgmental attitude.

SUGGESTED READING

Cochran, J. L., & Cochran, N. H. (2006). *The heart of counseling: A guide to developing therapeutic relationships.* Belmont, CA: Wadsworth.

Corey, M. S., & Corey, G. (2007). *Becoming a helper* (5th ed.). Belmont, CA: Wadsworth.

Deiro, J. A. (2004). *Teachers DO make a difference: The teacher's guide to connecting with students.* Thousand Oaks, CA: Corwin Press.

Gazda, G. M., Balzer, F. J., Childers, W. C., Nealy, A., Phelps, R. E., & Walters, R. P. (2005). *Human relations development: A manual for educators* (7th ed.). Boston: Allyn & Bacon.

Kottler, J. A., & Carlson, J. (2005). *Their finest hour: Master therapists share their greatest success stories.* Boston: Allyn & Bacon.

Sommers-Flanagan, J., & Sommers-Flanagan, R. (1997). *Tough kids, cool counseling: User-friendly approaches with challenging youth.* Alexandria, VA: American Counseling Association.

Welfel, E. R., & Patterson, L. E. (2005). *The counseling process: A multitheoretical integrative approach* (6th ed.). Belmont, CA: Wadsworth.

Assessing Children's Problems 3

Nick has his head down in the back of the room. Occasionally, you can see one of his eyes squint open for a moment before he sighs and burrows deeper into the cradle of his arms. As you continue the lesson, trying to concentrate on what you will do next, you can't help but worry about what is going on with this boy. Before you can sort out your thoughts on the matter, you catch the beginnings of an altercation developing on the other side of the room. Belinda keeps poking Teresa, who can't seem to stop giggling. The distraction seems to draw other kids' attention, and they are now becoming more and more restless—everyone, that is, except Nick, who remains immobile, frozen in position with only the top of his head showing.

You decide to abruptly change gears and give the class an assignment to complete; they weren't really listening to you anyway. Everyone dutifully takes out his or her paper and pen, opens the book to the proper page, and begins the exercise—everyone, that is, but Nick, who is either sleeping or lost in his own world.

You know you've got to do something about this. You're going to approach Nick, but before you do, you'd like to formulate some sort of idea about what might be going on. This is really so unlike him. Usually, he has a lot of energy; he's the first one to raise his hand. But now, something is terribly wrong—the kid looks beat.

You review the possibilities that immediately come to mind. After all, before you can do something to intervene, you must first have some notion about what the problem might be. Is he tired? That's the first thought that comes to mind. Maybe he's not sleeping well at night for some reason. It could be a family problem, or some dramatic change at home.

Another possibility occurs to you as well. Your intuition tells you that he looks depressed. You notice some of the signs: He seems lethargic and listless. Lately, he doesn't seem to take pleasure in anything. He strikes you as sad, maybe even lonely, but that could be your own take on things rather than the way he is really feeling. You wonder what his appetite has been like lately, whether he has experienced any recent trauma or disappointment, or whether he has any physical symptoms accompanying this blunted emotion.

Maybe you are not seeing depression or grief or sadness at all. It's entirely possible something else could be going on. Is he doing this for attention? Might this be a cry for help? He could be feeling more indifferent to school right now for some reason. Maybe he's just bored with what you're doing in class that day. Or possibly he could be composing a piece of music or writing a story in his head and doesn't want to be interrupted.

Well, you can speculate all you want, but the only way you're going to get a handle on Nick's behavior is to talk to him directly. You hope he'll tell you what's on his mind, or at least talk to the counselor about it. But before you decide what the best course of action might be, you need to assess the situation.

NOTICING SYMPTOMS OF DISTRESS

Assessment is an important part of a teacher's job. You have been taught to recognize a number of children's difficulties, including academic underachievement, cognitive deficits, learning disabilities, behavioral problems, and signs of child abuse. Yet these areas of difficulty represent, proportionately, only a small segment of what children struggle with in their daily lives. They are fighting to establish themselves as autonomous, confident, and competent human beings. They are working through a number of developmental transitions related to achieving physical, cognitive, emotional, and moral maturity. They are recovering from the stresses and strains of family and peer pressure, trying desperately to find a place in the world where they belong. They are trying to make a number of important life decisions about school, friends, work, and the future. And these are only the predictable and normal problems of adjustment that children encounter.

About one in five students in your classes is suffering from emotional difficulties not considered part of normal childhood adjustment. These children are highly anxious, so much so that they develop psychosomatic illnesses and stress-related symptoms, such as chronic headaches, stomachaches, ulcers, and insomnia. Depression is also quite common among school-age children, a condition that is often overlooked because these kids tend to be withdrawn, passive, and quiet—not the sort to draw attention to themselves. Some of these kids are potentially suicidal and spend an inordinate amount of time planning their own demise, all while staring blankly at the blackboard. Still other children are hiding symptoms of drug abuse or eating disorders.

You will, of course, already have noticed those who have the more dramatic signs of severe personality disorders, but the vast majority of children's problems are overlooked by teachers who are not trained to notice their warning signs.

STRESS IN THE LIVES OF CHILDREN

Throughout their lifespan, children are confronted with a number of stressors that make it far more challenging for them to master age-appropriate developmental tasks (see Table 3.1).

From the moment of birth, which is itself an incredibly stressful event, children are required to deal with a constant battery of new challenges, many of which seem beyond what they can manage comfortably. Unlike adults, who have at their disposal an array of coping mechanisms that

Table 3.1   Overview of Developmental Stages and Major Stressors

Stage	Age	Developmental Tasks	Major Stressors
Infancy	Birth–3 years	Learning to trust, mastering physical tasks of feeding, communicating, movement, talking, crawling, walking	Helpless to meet needs, body control, environmental obstacles
Early Childhood	3–6 years	Getting along with age-mates, learning social skills and roles, developing independence, controlling own behavior, learning gender role, learning right from wrong	Manage frustration, first conflicts, guilt, self-restraint
School Age	6–12 years	Developing sense of competence, learning basic values, learning to read, developing social circle, adapting to siblings, learning abstract reasoning	Feeling inferior, school and sports performance, emotional control, delay gratification
Adolescence	13–18 years	Developing identity, planning for future work, organizing time, understanding sexual orientation, peer roles	Social pressures, drugs, emotional volatility, hormonal changes
Early Adulthood	19–23 years	Developing intimacy, education and apprenticeship, career plans, learning to love, building friendships	Loneliness, sexuality, career confusion, financial independence

SOURCE: Adapted from Kottler, J. A., & Chen, D. (2008). *Stress management and prevention*. Belmont, CA: Wadsworth.

include greater mastery of their environment, more choices, and even prescription medications, young children are often at the mercy of things beyond their control. Parents, teachers, and older kids tell them what to do, when and how to do it, and then administer punishments if performance does not meet expectations.

There are a number of early signs of stress overload among young children, some of which include bed-wetting, weight gain, withdrawal, isolation, acting-out, sudden and unexplained fears, recklessness, emotional outbursts, unexplained physical problems, avoidance, aggressive or violent behavior, escapism in television and computer games, and even drugs, which may begin as young as seven or eight years of age.

Adolescence brings even more serious developmental challenges to accompany hormonal and bodily changes and social pressures. This is a time in life in which people experience the most varied and stressful life difficulties adjusting to pressures at home, in school, among friends, and with family. In addition to all the evidence of dysfunction just mentioned in the context of younger children, adolescents have to deal with temptations to indulge in drinking, drugs, eating disorders, promiscuous sex, and gangs, all of which provide temporary relief even if they have negative side effects.

During the assessment process, your job is not merely to note the presence of stress in children's lives, which is pervasive and unavoidable, but rather to make determinations of when the level and duration are beyond what can be reasonably tolerated. Some children rise to the challenges presented by stress and grow stronger as a result; others surrender, or engage in self-destructive behaviors that will come to your attention—*if* you know what to look for.

THE ASSESSMENT PROCESS

The most critical component of any treatment plan designed to help children in need is to assess accurately the nature of their difficulties. Assume, for instance, that a child sits quietly in class, rarely contributing to discussions. His eyes are downcast, his posture slumped. He almost never interacts with other children, nor has he ever engaged you in any conversation. Does this child have an emotional problem, and, if so, what is its nature?

That is a very good question indeed, and one without a definitive answer. This child's behavior could mean any number of things—he is chronically shy, he is depressed, he feels alienated and lonely, he suffers from an autistic or schizoid disorder in which he is disconnected from the human race, he is on drugs or overmedicated, he has been kept up at night and is tired, perhaps, even, he is a member of a culture in which his behavior is considered socially appropriate. Each of these possible diagnoses would suggest a different method of intervention and a different professional whom you might consult for help.

It is not enough to sense that something is wrong with a child; you must also have a rough idea of what is going on before you can take appropriate action, whether that is to contact parents, social welfare, the school counselor, a physician, or someone else.

This process of systematically observing behavior, determining if it indicates some underlying difficulty, narrowing down the possibilities to a few reasonable hypotheses, and then initiating some form of action resembles the differential diagnostic methods of physicians and psychologists. Your job is to figure out if, indeed, there is a serious problem and, if so, what to do about it.

Essentially, you will be asking yourself a series of questions:

- What is unusual about this child's behavior?
- Is there a pattern to what you have observed?
- What information do you need to make an informed judgment?
- Whom might you contact to collect this background?
- What are the risks of waiting longer to figure out what is going on?
- Does this child seem to be in any immediate danger?
- What can you do to build a better relationship with the child?

It is certainly beyond the scope of your role as a teacher to be able to diagnose accurately a host of emotional disorders, differentiate them from one another, and then prescribe corresponding treatments. It is perfectly reasonable that with added training and supervised experience, you would become proficient in recognizing some of the signs of a child who is in trouble. You will, however, want to be very careful to avoid labeling kids based on only a few samples of their behavior. Even when they're accurate, diagnoses have a habit of following people around for a long time, leading to future biases: For example, once labeled "emotionally disturbed," "hyperactive," "learning disabled," or "oppositional/defiant," it's very difficult to get rid of that name. In other words, we caution you that although failing to identify some evidence of emotional problem is a serious lapse, it is almost as devastating to play "amateur shrink" and assign diagnoses to children based on limited information and training.

COLLECTING ADDITIONAL INFORMATION

Once your attention is drawn to a child who appears to be exhibiting evidence of underlying difficulties and is in need of help, the next step is to collect more information through observation and further research. This information can be collected in several ways.

- Talk to the student's teacher from the previous year to get some basis for comparison with what you observe.
- Consult with other teachers and staff in the school who have worked with the child.
- Learn more about the child's identified culture to find out if the behavior you observe is normative.
- Review available school records.
- Talk to the child's friends to get their impressions of what might be going on.
- Schedule a conference with parents to discover what occurs at home.
- The most obvious course of action is to talk to the student directly and let him or her know that you are concerned.

Without training or preparation, it is difficult to know what you are observing or what you have discovered, other than the fact that a child appears troubled. We will review some of the more common disorders and difficulties that you will encounter, list the most prevalent symptoms you might observe, and then mention the usual treatment strategies so that you can take appropriate action or make informed referrals.

In conducting any assessment process, counselors and psychologists usually follow a process in which they attempt to do the following:

1. Familiarize themselves with the child's world, including dominant culture, family history, and current living situation

2. Check out the child's strengths and weaknesses with regard to intellectual, academic, emotional, interpersonal, moral, and behavioral functioning

3. Identify all presenting problems, not just those that are immediately obvious but also others that might be disguised, denied, or hidden from view

4. Formulate a diagnostic impression that includes acute symptoms, identified stressors that might be contributing to the problem, characteristic personality style, physical complaints that might be relevant, and level of adaptive functioning

5. Develop a treatment plan to reach mutually agreed-upon goals

Although you won't be involved in many of the stages of this assessment procedure, it is important to understand the way the process works. In all likelihood, you will be asked to provide important background information and observations that will be useful to the professional who works with a given case.

As you review each of these types of emotional problems, consider how you would go through each of the steps just presented.

Grief and Loss

Description

Although it is normal and appropriate for children to experience a disturbed mood as a result of a loss, whether through death, divorce, trauma, tragedy, or life transition, prolonged and chronic disturbance requires intervention.

Example

A child's grandmother dies after a sudden illness. The child was especially close to this family member, who had caretaking responsibility. After an initial period of observed sadness, the child began to progressively deteriorate, even after several months, losing interest in school and friends.

Symptoms

Pathological grief is characterized by disruptive symptoms that last many months. They included sleep disruption, listlessness, depression, appetite loss, somatic symptoms (headaches, stomachaches, nausea, intestinal problems, and so on), confusion, nightmares, numbness, fears, and acting-out behavior.

Usual Interventions

A supportive, trusting relationship is needed to help the child explore and express unresolved feelings. It is important that the child is encouraged to talk about the loss, but helped not to dwell on it. Children are often helped to understand that when people die you don't actually "lose" them but rather you negotiate a different kind of relationship, one in which they continue to "live" in your heart and mind.

Generalized Anxiety

Description

Excessive worry and apprehension over things that are out of one's control or in which the reaction is exaggerated beyond what is reasonable.

Example

A child agonizes continuously over school, sports, and social performance. He expresses persistent concern over possible harm that may befall his parents and so is reluctant to separate from them. Another common example is test anxiety, in which a student's performance becomes seriously impaired because of disturbing thoughts.

Symptoms

Nausea, stomachaches, headaches, sweating, dry mouth, frequent urination, dizziness, agitation, restlessness, irritability.

Usual Interventions

Give lots of reassurance, use relaxation training and stress management, provide an opportunity to talk about fears and learn alternative ways to handle them, refer for counseling, make a referral to rule out associated physical maladies. In the case of test anxiety, structure the environment to minimize stress.

Phobic Disorders

Description

Avoidant and anxious responses to specific situations, such as being in open spaces (agoraphobia); separation from a parent (separation anxiety); social situations (social phobia); or spiders, snakes, high places, and so on (simple phobia).

Example

A child develops a persistent refusal to go to school after an embarrassing experience. She refuses to leave her parent's side when she is forcibly dragged away from home.

Symptoms

Persistent fears, physical sensations (sweating, heart palpitations, trembling, nausea, numbness, dizziness), avoidance of threatening stimuli.

Usual Interventions

Teachers will want to work very closely with a therapist who can design a treatment program containing cognitive and behavioral components. Family counseling may be indicated. In school phobia cases, gradual desensitization is introduced. Teachers can be helpful by creating a supportive atmosphere.

Post-Traumatic Stress

Description

Incapacitation or diminished functioning as a result of some horrific experience (victim of violence, natural disaster, sexual abuse, robbery, kidnapping, serious accident).

Example

A child returns home from school one day to discover his father's body on the floor, the victim of a sudden heart attack. The child becomes more and more aloof after this incident, eventually appearing nonresponsive and unemotional in response to anything around him.

Symptoms

Reliving of the traumatic event over and over at least one month after the incident, sleep and eating disruptions, drastic change in behavior, withdrawal, difficulties with concentration or completing tasks, startle responses, memory deficits.

Usual Interventions

Lots of patience, support, and reassurance are needed. Teachers should refer the child to a counselor or therapist for ongoing care, usually in conjunction with family therapy. Teachers can help by strengthening support systems in school and providing the child with a safe, predictable environment.

Depression

Description

A pervasive mood disorder in which the child feels sad and withdrawn, with muted feelings. There are several different kinds of depression: *endogenous depression* is a biologically based disorder that is caused by a neurochemical imbalance in the body; *dysthymia* is another chronic but less serious mood disorder in which there is no serious disruption of sleep, appetite, or daily functioning; *reactive depression* is an acute response to some crisis or distressing situation (grief, adjustment to life changes, and so on), that is not quite so extreme as to warrant diagnosis as posttraumatic stress.

Example

A child has recently moved to the district from another city. He appears very quiet, reticent, and withdrawn. Sometimes you can see tears welling up in his eyes. He usually keeps to himself and does not initiate interaction with other children.

Symptoms

In mild cases: sadness following an identifiable stressful event that precipitated the symptoms, low energy, poor concentration, low self-esteem, no history of recurrent episodes. In severe cases: disruption of normal functioning, appetite loss, sleep disruption, weight loss or gain, listlessness, withdrawal, abject hopelessness, rumination, suicidal thoughts and possible intent. Also, look for signs of alcohol or drug use.

Usual Interventions

Mild, reactive depression responds quite well to supportive relationships in which the child has the opportunity to express feelings and learn alternative ways of thinking about his or her predicament. Time is usually the best healer.

Chronic, low-grade depression (dysthymia) is much more challenging to treat. Therapists usually try a combination of supportive relationships with cognitive restructuring methods. Teachers can help by making an early referral before the symptoms become more serious and intractable.

Severe endogenous depression, on the other hand, is potentially life threatening without intervention. In some cases, intensive psychotherapy in addition to medication is required. The teacher can play a crucial role by making sure that the child does receive expert help. As with all of these situations, when making referrals, express caring and concern for the child and let him know that you will follow up to make sure he got the help he needs.

Suicide Potential

Although it is not uncommon for children (and adults) to contemplate suicide during times of stress, here are some specific warning signs to watch for that indicate the potential for serious intent:

1. The end of the school year (when risks increase)

2. Use of drugs or alcohol

3. Extensive preoccupation with death fantasies

4. Absence of a support system

5. A specific plan as to how the child would do it

6. Available means to carry out the plan (a loaded gun or bottle of sleeping pills in the home)

7. A history of self-destructive acts

8. A gesture on the part of the child that may be interpreted as a cry for help

9. A history of a relative having killed him- or herself (providing a model of an acceptable way out)

10. Significant mood changes from depression to elation

11. Noticeable changes in a child's appearance or academic performance

It is also important to keep in mind that urban children are at greater risk than rural children, and certain minority groups (such as Native Americans) have higher than average suicide rates.

Prevention is critically important. Teachers can be most helpful by creating an atmosphere in their classes in which everyone is responsible for everyone else's welfare. Almost 90 percent of children who attempt suicide (or acts of violence) tell somebody of their intent—a friend, a parent, a teacher. By alerting children to the risk, we can recruit their assistance in preventing tragedy. Keep in mind, however, that predicting suicidal acts is not an exact science; it is better to be cautious and conservative when you suspect that a child is at risk, and consult a counselor.

Teachers are sometimes involved in systematic programs to deal with the aftermath of suicide in a school, a potentially devastating event for the survivors, who often receive very little attention. As with any other tragedy that occurs, teachers should spend some time in class allowing children to talk about their reactions and then providing time for discussion. After closure has been reached in a reasonable period of time, efforts should then be made to redirect the focus back to the scheduled lessons. This is important to provide a sense of continuity, sending the message that life goes on even in the face of terrible tragedies.

Attention-Deficit Hyperactivity Disorder

Description

High degrees of impulsivity, unrestrained energy, and inattention that are not typical for the age of the child. The behavior is manifested in a number of settings, in school as well as at home, and seriously impairs the child's ability to concentrate or perform assigned tasks.

Example

A child is performing poorly in school in spite of an apparent high degree of intelligence. She almost always appears restless, practically vibrating with energy as her attention wanders from one thing to another without pause. The more concentration that is required for a particular task in school, the more frustrated she becomes.

Symptoms

Restless or fidgeting behavior, difficulty staying in one place for a period of time, easily distracted, impulsive behavior in class, attention wandering from assigned tasks that are rarely completed, excessive talking or constant interruptions of others, difficulty listening to and following instructions.

Usual Interventions

Structured individual assignments that are within the child's threshold of attentiveness, tight external boundaries, and medication for severe cases are usual interventions. In general, children work on developing appropriate social skills and positive attitudes.

Conduct Disorder

Description

A persistent pattern of abusing the rights of others with little regard for established rules. This child will appear unduly aggressive, even cruel in his or her destructive, violent, or antisocial behavior.

Example

A child explodes with temper tantrums when he does not get his way. He is provocative and seems oblivious to other children's feelings. He is often discovered to be starting fights, stealing others' things, or doing anything to get his way. Furthermore, he shows no guilt or remorse over his actions. He feels entitled to get his way whenever he wants and views others as his personal slaves.

Symptoms

A pattern of cruelty toward animals or age mates; participation in frequent fights; deliberate destruction of others' property; initiation of aggressive acts, either alone or as a leader of others.

Usual Interventions

Set very strict boundaries with immediate enforcement of consequences for noncompliance; improve frustration tolerance through gradual presentation of more challenging tasks; initiate family counseling to work on consistent parenting; use inpatient treatment for severe cases.

Oppositional Disorder

Description

A less severe version of a conduct disorder in which the child shows a pattern of being hostile, defiant, and uncooperative. This behavior is not necessarily universal but may appear only in certain settings (at home, in certain classes, when around certain people, in response to certain stimuli). The child does show some concern for others' rights and does not deliberately hurt others in attempts to protect him- or herself.

Example

A child appears surly, hostile, even ferocious in her opposition to you and things you ask of her. When you ask her to do something, she refuses outright, or sometimes even does the exact opposite. You can hear her swear at you behind your back and feel her disdain for you and everything for which you stand.

Symptoms

Frequent loss of temper; situational arguments with authority figures; a pattern of defiance, vindictiveness, and annoying others; common swearing and dramatic rebellion.

Usual Interventions

Set limits and enforce them without retribution; examine your own contributions to precipitating the oppositional behavior, because you are also part of the conflict; schedule individual conferences to confront the behavior nondefensively and work on a more empathic alliance. Unlike children suffering from conduct disorders, these children respond quite well to a teacher's systematic attempts to improve self-esteem, frustration tolerance, emotional control, and aggression. They also respond well to counseling because they must develop cooperative relationships with an authority figure during the process.

Eating Disorders

Description

A disturbance in eating behavior characterized by significant weight loss and obsession with food (anorexia nervosa); episodes of bingeing and forced vomiting (bulimia); or persistent eating of innutritious substances such as paint, chalk, plaster, paper, leaves, and so on (pica).

Example

You have noticed that one of the girls in your class is as "skinny as a rail," yet you have occasionally overheard her remark to friends how fat she is. She has low self-esteem. You recall that she was once much heavier and began to lose weight after her relationship with a boyfriend ended.

Symptoms

The prevalence of anorexia nervosa and bulimia occurs almost exclusively among girls, especially in adolescence; perfectionist behavior; mild obesity before onset of weight loss; excessive concern for food but poor eating habits; distorted body image.

Usual Interventions

Because in virtually all cases the child's friends and family know about her unusual eating habits, teachers can do a lot to educate children on the signs of trouble and the dangerous consequences of these disorders. In severe cases, eating disorders are potentially lethal without hospitalization. In more moderate cases, family counseling and behavior modification are often successful.

Schizophrenia

Description

A distinct distortion of reality in the presence of hallucinations, delusions, or bizarre behavior. Although other diagnoses are possible (brief psychotic reaction) depending on duration of symptoms and subtle variations, you will notice fairly marked deviations from normal functioning.

Example

An adolescent girl has been acting progressively more bizarre in school. Other children shy away from her and make fun of her; she seems oblivious to their teasing, to anything, really. She speaks in nonsensical phrases, stares blankly out the window, and claims that she sometimes hears voices.

Symptoms

Presence of unusual behavior for at least one week; the presence of delusions or hallucinations; incoherent and disconnected speech; inappropriate emotional reactions; strange, delusional beliefs; social withdrawal; peculiar behavior.

Usual Interventions

The sooner intervention takes place, the more favorable the prognosis; conversely, the longer the symptoms go on, the more likely the child will not fully recover. Treatment usually consists of brief hospitalization, medication to control delusional thinking, and psychotherapy to help the child readjust. Because early detection is so crucial to recovery, teachers can be instrumental in helping the child by referring him or her for professional help.

Substance Abuse Disorders

Description

The addiction to, dependence on, or habitual use of alcohol, marijuana, cocaine, barbiturates, amphetamines, or other substances to the extent that normal functioning is impaired.

Example

A child in your class repeatedly falls asleep and appears lethargic when he is awake. His eyes sometimes appear glassy, his speech slurred. There has been a noticeable change in his behavior and academic performance over the course of several weeks. You happen to know that the friends with whom he has been hanging around are regular users of drugs and alcohol.

Symptoms

Frequent use of a psychoactive substance in increasing amounts; little control over the amount and frequency of the substance that is ingested; a lot of time spent thinking about the drug; disruption of social and school activities; impairment in functioning that may be manifested in slurred speech, shaky gait, glassy or bloodshot eyes, irritability, hyperactivity, or lethargy.

Usual Interventions

A supportive relationship with a teacher can be a catalyst for a student to break away from self-destructive habits. The treatment of these problems is very difficult because the problems involve both a physical habit or addiction and social reinforcement among one's peer group. Referral to a specialist in substance abuse disorders is usually indicated because the child may need fairly drastic disruption of his or her usual life routines in order to recover fully. Brief hospitalization is often suggested, along with family counseling, individual counseling, and reeducation. Prevention is by far the best treatment, and teachers play a major role in addressing the risks before behavior gets out of hand.

Obsessive-Compulsive Disorder

Description

Recurrent thoughts (obsessions) or repetitive behaviors (compulsions) beyond one's control. They are usually senseless ideas or actions that represent attempts to ward off other concerns through ritualistic action.

Example

A child meticulously arranges every aspect of her desk before she will attempt any project. She is insistent that everything be absolutely in its correct place and refuses to do any work unless everything is in order. She rarely completes any of her work because of her inordinate concern for arranging materials.

Symptoms

Repetitive behavior or recurrent thoughts that keep anxiety under control, images or impulses that are intrusive and render the person at least minimally dysfunctional.

Usual Interventions

The earlier the obsessive thinking or compulsive behavior is detected, the greater the likelihood that it can be treated. Behavior therapy is the preferred intervention; medication is also sometimes effective.

Somatization Disorder

Description

A long-standing series of physical complaints without any apparent organic cause. This disorder represents the body's attempt to metabolize stress. The child is distressed by the symptoms and is not faking them.

Example

A child constantly complains of stomachaches. He has been taken to a number of specialists but they have found no cause for the trouble.

Symptoms

Preoccupation with some problem in the body for which there is no known physical cause. Common symptoms include abdominal pain, back pain, or headaches.

Usual Interventions

Rule out completely the possibility of any medical condition; focus on improving functioning in school and with friends rather than on symptoms themselves; employ stress reduction strategies, as well as individual and/or family therapy to explore sources of anxiety.

Factitious Disorder

Description

Intentional manufacture of physical problems to gain attention or sympathy, assume a sick role, or escape some obligation.

Example

A child has missed a lot of school because of illnesses. One day, she complained of stomach pains and wished to go home. You told her to wait a little while to see if she felt any better. You then caught her secretly trying to make herself vomit.

Symptoms

A persistent pattern of deliberately feigned physical symptoms; a personality that is demanding and manipulative; a high need for attention.

Usual Interventions

Eliminate consequences that the child is enjoying as a result of malingering; refer to individual and family therapy to get at sources of need for attention.

Sexual Abuse

Description

The incidence of sexual abuse has been estimated as high as 25 percent of all girls; although the frequency is less among boys, it is still a major problem. Most of these occurrences go unreported and significantly affect a child's self-esteem, development, and school performance. Obviously, this child is also at greater risk for having relationship problems in the future.

Example

A child cringes when you softly touch her arm to offer comfort. You have observed that is her usual response to any male who comes too close to her.

Symptoms

Fear of adults, especially own parents; reluctance to go home; withdrawal or regressive behavior; complaints of frequent nightmares; secretiveness about family life; reported stories of being touched inappropriately.

Usual Interventions

Suspected sexual abuse must be reported to the authorities, triggering an investigation; treatment usually consists of family therapy, with separate treatment for the perpetrator(s); teachers are instrumental in helping the child develop a safe, trusting relationship with a caring adult; the child is usually seen in individual counseling to work on issues related to betrayal, self-esteem, and accompanying guilt.

Personality Disorders

Description

A relatively enduring, stable set of characteristics that is considered maladaptive. This person usually appears odd (paranoid, schizoid disorders); dramatic and unpredictable (borderline, narcissistic, histrionic, antisocial disorders); or anxious and fearful (avoidant, passive-aggressive, or dependent disorders).

Example

A child has a consistent pattern of lying, theft, truancy, drug abuse, and cruelty to others. He is amoral and irresponsible, responding to nothing that you or anyone else can do to control his behavior.

Symptoms

Behavior on the part of a child that is an extension of his or her personality, self-defeating, and quite dysfunctional in daily life.

Usual Interventions

The prognosis for these disorders is generally not very good. Because the traits are long-standing and stable, they are resistant to change. These are the children who will consistently give you the most trouble in class. Intensive, long-term individual psychotherapy is usually prescribed, sometimes in addition to group and family therapy. Many times, the teacher will need professional consultation in order to work with these children so that they don't disrupt class functioning.

Adjustment Disorders

Description

Stressful reactions to some recent event in the child's life (such as family death, relocation, illness, or relationship problem). The nature of the reaction is more moderate than that of post-traumatic stress described earlier.

Example

Formerly a cheerful and very good student, a child became surly, uncooperative, and withdrawn after being informed that his parents were getting a divorce. He appeared sad.

Symptoms

Anxiety, depression, withdrawal, behavioral changes, physical complaints, or reduced academic performance immediately following an identifiable stressful event in the child's life.

Usual Interventions

These are the kinds of difficulties that respond best to a teacher's empathic concern. The majority of children will improve on their own if provided the time and opportunity to do so. Referral to a counselor can hasten the recovery period, as can participation in support groups. Teachers can often be of tremendous assistance in providing a setting for children to talk about what is bothering them and to feel understood.

Most often, teachers will see this last category of problems. Fortunately, these emotional concerns are also the kinds of difficulties that respond best to a teacher moderately skilled in helping strategies.

WHAT TO DO WITH THE ASSESSMENT

Once you have generated some hypotheses about what might be going on with a student like Nick (the young man who began this chapter), who seems to be experiencing some type of emotional problem, the next step is to plan some sort of helping strategy. There are a number of issues you will wish to consider:

- Does this child appear to be in imminent danger that requires immediate, decisive action?
- Is this student at risk of hurting him- or herself or someone else?
- Is this the type of problem that you can handle yourself, or should you make a referral to someone else?

- If a referral is indicated, whom should you consult first? The counselor? School psychologist? School social worker? Special education teacher? Principal?
- If you are going to handle this situation yourself, at least initially, what would be the best approach to take with this particular child?

The last question is one that forces you to consider the individual characteristics as well as the cultural background of the child you are assessing. The counseling skills you will learn in the next chapter will be adapted for each unique student, depending on what is needed and what is likely to prove most helpful at that moment in time.

SUGGESTED ACTIVITIES

1. Do a complete assessment of yourself, including academic, educational, vocational, social, family, and personality factors. Note what you learned from this systematic effort to study your own development. How did this process help you identify clearer goals for yourself?

2. Interview a partner and attempt to create a comprehensive assessment of his or her strengths and weaknesses in several specific areas. After reviewing your notes, identify several key themes that seemed to emerge. Present the results of this analysis to your partner and then help him or her process reactions to the feedback.

3. Survey your friends. In what ways could teachers have been more helpful to them while growing up?

SUGGESTED READING

Capuzzi, D., & Gross, D. (2005). *Youth at risk: A prevention resource for counselors, teachers, and parents* (4th ed.). Alexandria, VA: American Counseling Association.

Fiorini, J. J., & Mullen, J. A. (2006). *Counseling children and adolescents through grief and loss.* Champaign, IL: Research Press.

Haslam, R. H., & Valletutti, P. J. (Eds.). (2004). *Medical problems in the classroom: The teacher's role in diagnosis and management* (4th ed). Austin, TX: Pro-Ed.

Jensen, P. S., Knapp, P., & Mrazek, D. A. (2006). *Toward a new diagnostic system for child psychopathology: Moving beyond the DSM.* New York: Guilford.

Kottler, J. A., & Chen, D. (2008). *Stress management and prevention.* Belmont, CA: Wadsworth.

McWhirter, J. J., McWhirter, B. T., McWhirter, E. H., & McWhirter, R. J. (2007). *At-risk youth: A comprehensive response for counselors, teachers, psychologists, and human services professionals.* Belmont, CA: Wadsworth.

Seligman, L. (2004). *Diagnosis and treatment planning in counseling* (3rd ed.). New York: Springer.

Wilmshurst, L. (2003). *Child and adolescent psychopathology: A casebook.* Thousand Oaks, CA: Sage.

Developing Skills of Helping

4

Although the focus of our discussion now turns to the skills of responding to children in a helpful capacity, much of your success in these endeavors will depend on things you do inside your own head before the conversation even begins. Counseling encounters are different from other human interactions because of your state of mind as you enter the relationship. Counseling is, in a way, a form of meditation in which both participants are concentrating intently on what the other is saying; it is as if nothing or nobody else exists outside the circle of their interaction.

Counselors and therapists often are accused of being able to read minds when, in fact, what they are doing is simply focusing all their attention, all their energy—their very *being*—on what the others are saying, doing, and meaning by their words or gestures. With such full and complete attention toward others, it is indeed possible to anticipate what people will say next and even what they are thinking; sometimes this occurs before they have fully articulated these ideas to themselves.

Before you begin a counseling encounter, it is extremely important to take steps to clear your mind of all distractions, to put aside your own worries, your grumbling stomach, the tasks you must complete later in the day. In yoga, meditation, martial arts, or any contemplative art (of which counseling is certainly a part), participants are encouraged to take a *cleansing breath* before they begin their activity. A deep breath helps clear yourself of muddled and distracting thoughts and helps "center" yourself on the interaction that is about to begin. This breath comes to symbolize the commitment that you are making to the student, that for the next few minutes nothing exists except your interest and caring for him or her. If you experiment with this kind of attitude in other relationships in your life, you will notice a remarkable change taking place in the quality and intimacy of your interactions.

Beginning counseling students often report both miraculous and annoying changes in their interactions with loved ones. On the one hand, they notice that they become involved in much deeper and richer conversations. People in their lives are so appreciative of the added attention they are receiving. Yet on the other hand, when the attending and listening efforts are clumsy and contrived (as they will sometimes be in the beginning) friends and family members might complain that you are doing "that counseling stuff." What they really mean by that is that they are not used to being listened to with such attention and concentration. Perhaps you'll agree this is quite sad.

INTERNAL STATE OF MIND

Once you have cleared your mind and focused your concentration, the next imperative is that you monitor your internal attitudes. Counselors are helpful precisely because they are perceived as being nonjudgmental, accepting, and noncritical. Outside of the helping encounter, you could easily feel critical toward what you are hearing, but once you have made a decision to function in a helping role, you suspend temporarily that part of you that judges others. After all, critical evaluations interfere with your ability to respond compassionately to what you are hearing. If the student senses even a little bit of authoritarian criticism on your part, all trust can be lost.

If we could enter the mind of a teacher who is struggling to monitor critical thoughts that take place during a conversation with a student, this is what we might hear in the way of internal dialogue:

I can't believe she could be so stupid . . .

Oops. Deep breath. She's just doing the best she can and doesn't know any better.

But how can she have been so clueless as to . . .

There I go again. Find my compassion. Breathe. Remember that she lives in a different world than I do. This has worked for her before so she's doing it again.

If she were my *kid, I wouldn't tolerate this for a minute . . .*

But I'm not *her parent. I'm her teacher. I can't do anything about what is out of my control. All I can do is to support her, to set limits and enforce them. Just listen. Really listen to what she's saying. Nobody ever listens to her. They just judge her and tell her what to do. And I want to do the same thing.*

Just as it takes many months of disciplined practice to master any meditative state, so too does it require lots of practice to keep yourself as clearheaded, noncritical, and compassionate as you can while you are listening and responding to students in need. In this initial stage of making contact with a child, before you even open your mouth to say anything or apply your first helping skill, you are already setting in motion an internal state of mind, a set of helping attitudes, to help yourself be maximally receptive and responsive to what you will hear. You will remind yourself to stay flexible, push aside distractions, and feel compassionate toward what is about to take place.

ATTENDING

Easier than it may sound, appearing attentive to children is the first and most basic task in being helpful. If you would simply monitor yourself and others during most interactions, you would notice how rare it is that people are being fully attentive to one another. While addressing you, and purportedly listening, a friend is also probably engaged in a number of simultaneous activities—looking over your shoulder, waving to someone walking by, rustling through papers, or grooming hair. Such divided behavior hardly inspires your confidence, nor does it communicate that you are all that important to that person during that moment in time.

Practice Attending and Listening

Get together with a partner (classmate, friend, or family member) and ask that person to talk to you about something going on in his or her life. Your job during this practice exercise is not to speak but just to listen as carefully and completely as you possibly can. You are to indicate through nonverbal cues that you are following the conversation, especially using head nods, eye contact, facial expressions, and body posture. You can also use verbal encouragers ("uh-huh," "I see," "go on") to keep things going.

As well as your nonverbal attending and listening skills, monitor what is going on within you as well. Really *listen* to what the person is saying—hear not just the surface words but pay attention to the underlying meaning of the messages. Throughout the few minutes of this exercise, try to feel as much empathy and compassion as you can. Remember that your job is not to fix anything, nor even to *say* anything, but just to "hold" this person with your interest and attention.

Attending to someone means giving him or her your total, complete, and undivided interest. It means using your body, your face, your eyes—yes, especially your eyes—to say, "Nothing exists right now for me except you. Every ounce of my energy and being is focused on you."

You would be truly amazed at how healing this simple act can be—giving another person your full attention. Children, in particular, are often so used to being devalued by adults that attending behaviors instantly tell them that something is different about this interaction: "Here is a person who seems to care about me and what I have to say."

You might check out the power of simple attending skills in your relationships with friends and family. The next time you speak to someone you care about, make a commitment to give him or her your undivided attention. Resist all distractions. Face the person fully. Maintain continual eye contact. Use your face and body to communicate your intense interest in what is being said. Afterward, ask the person if they noticed any difference in the way you appeared or how it felt.

LISTENING

Attending skills involve the use of nonverbal behaviors (head nods, smiles, eye contact, body positions) and minimal verbal encouragement ("uh-huh," "I see") to communicate your intense interest in what a person is saying. Although these skills are a requirement to earn a person's trust, they are relatively empty gestures unless you are actually listening and can prove that you have understood.

This presents an interesting challenge: How do you demonstrate to people that you understand them? How do you show them that you not only heard what they said, but you really know what they mean?

There are two ways to show evidence of such synchronized attention: *passive listening*, which we have already described in the context of nonverbal and verbal attending, and *active listening*, in which you take a more direct role in responding to what you heard. Ultimately, listening is communicated by the way you respond to the speaker, by your ability to prove that you really did hear what has been said.

Student: *"I just don't get this assignment. It seems stupid and doesn't make any sense why we're even doing it in the first place."*

Teacher: *"You're really frustrated and don't see the point of this. You came to talk to me about this because you'd really like to understand better what I had in mind."*

Note how the teacher does not become defensive, does not explain the assignment at this point, but simply demonstrates that she heard what the student was saying to her.

EMPATHIC RESONANCE

Empathy is the ability (and willingness) to crawl inside someone else's skin and to grasp another person's experience. This is when attending, listening, and interpersonal sensitivity come together in such a way that you are able to get outside yourself enough that you can sense what the other person is feeling and thinking.

The second part of this helping behavior involves communicating your understanding of what you hear/see/sense/feel in such a way that the student does not feel quite so alone. If we put all the skills together that have been presented so far—including attending, listening, and empathic resonance—ideally, you would structure a conversation in which the student feels encouraged to explore things. One such dialogue will be illustrated below with a student who is upset about a poor grade she received on an exam:

Student: *"You gave me a D on this test."* (Said accusingly, with tears in her eyes)

Teacher: (Puts down papers she was grading. Turns her chair to face the student fully. Softens her face and waits patiently [attending].) *"Yes, that's true. You did earn a D on the exam."* [Note the way in which the statement is reworded—placing emphasis on the student's responsibility.]

Student: *"Well, I don't think that's right! This test wasn't fair."*

Teacher: (Nods head [attending]) *"You don't think the test covered the stuff you had prepared for."* [Note that the teacher didn't take the bait and get into an argument over the content; instead, using active listening, the focus remained on what the student thought and felt.]

Student: *"Well, it didn't. And now my parents will kill me."*

Teacher: *"You sound more concerned about your parents' reaction than you do about the test itself."* [Empathic resonance allowed the teacher to ignore the part about the test and zoom in on the fear of parents' reactions.]

Student: *"They just expect so much from me."*

Teacher: (Nods her head [attending]. Smiles reassuringly [passive listening].) *"Yes, I can see how difficult this is for you. You are really feeling under a lot of pressure."* [Empathic resonance]

As is evident from this helping encounter, these first counseling skills are connected to one another in that they all attempt to build an open, trusting, and accepting atmosphere in which the student feels comfortable disclosing and exploring her feelings. The teacher stops what she is doing and turns her attention and her body to the student. This style is very unnatural for teachers who are used to dispensing advice, quickly solving problems, and multitasking. Instead, your goal in this initial stage is to be a perfect listener while you collect information, help the student to feel comfortable, and build trust in your relationship.

EXPLORATION SKILLS

This next set of skills is intended to help you build on what you have already begun with active listening. In addition to attending fully to the person, hearing the nuances in what is being said, decoding underlying meanings in communication, and acknowledging that you understood the meanings, the next step is to explore further the nature of the concerns.

Questioning

Certainly, the most obvious and direct way to gather information or encourage students to explore a particular area is to ask them a series of questions. As you read the previous dialogue, probably a number of ideas came to mind: Why do you feel the test was unfair? How much time did you spend studying for the test? How are you doing in your other classes? What will your parents do when they find out? What do your parents expect of you?

The problem with questions, as naturally as they may come to mind, is that they often put the child in a "one down" position in which you are the interrogator and expert problem solver. The message is communicated: Tell me what the situation is, and I will fix it for you. For that reason, questions are used only when you can't get the student to reveal information in other ways. You would be amazed at how much territory you can cover by relying on other, more indirect methods of exploration.

If you must ask questions, word them in such a way that they are *open ended*, or the kind that can't be answered with a single word, as opposed to *close ended*, or those that can be satisfied with a one-word response. Contrast the differences in the following examples:

Close Ended	Open Ended
Are you feeling upset now?	*What are you feeling right now?*
Are you going to tell your parents?	*What are you going to do?*
Did you have a good class today?	*How was class today?*

It is fairly obvious that open-ended questions encourage further exploration, whereas close-ended queries tend to cut off communication. You may end up with the answer to your question but at the expense of prolonged silences in which the child is waiting for you to continue directing the course of the conversation.

One notable exception to the rule of avoiding questions whenever possible, especially close-ended ones, is when it is important to gather very specific information in a potentially threatening or dangerous situation. For example, if a child expressed suicidal thoughts, it would be very appropriate to ask specific questions: Have you ever tried it before? Do you have a plan for how you would do it? Do you have the means to carry out your plan? Will you promise me that you won't do anything until we can get you some help? A "yes" response to the first three questions and "no" to the last would signal the need to take some definite preventive action beyond the scope of merely reflecting the child's feelings.

The Hot Seat

One fun activity to try in class, or even with friends, is to take turns asking open-ended questions that are designed to elicit the most personal, revealing information possible. The person on the "hot seat" agrees to answer any question asked as honestly as possible. People then take turns asking the kinds of questions that really encourage a person to think, and the nature of which tend to get unrehearsed answers. A good rule of thumb is to ask only the kinds of questions such that the answers you get would give you enough information about the essence of that person so that you could give a speech about him or her for 15 minutes. In other words, stay away from superficial, predictable questions and try to ask those that will really get the person to reveal a lot.

Here are some samples to get you started:

- What are you most proud of, and most ashamed of, in your life?
- When you escape into a fantasy during times that you're bored or anxious, where do you go?
- What's one thing about yourself that you most wish you could change?
- What's the one question you're most afraid I might ask?

Of course, before you ask questions like this, you'll want to be prepared to answer them yourself.

Reflecting Content

An indirect way to help someone further explore his or her concerns is to use your listening and empathy skills to reflect the *content* of what he or she is saying. This does not mean that you should sound like a parrot; rather, it indicates through rewording that you heard accurately what was said. These restatements help people clarify further what they are saying and facilitate additional exploration into the issues.

Student: *"Mikey keeps hitting me. He won't leave me alone and teases me all the time."*

Teacher: *"Mikey won't get off your back no matter what you do."*

In this simple reflection of content, the teacher acknowledges what was heard and also guides the focus toward the child's own behavior ("no matter what you do"). This might sound like a rather simple thing to do, but it is one of the most common skills employed by therapists and counselors because of the way it both encourages further expression and, at the same time, lets the other person know that you heard and understood what was communicated.

Reflecting Feelings

This skill is quite similar to the previous one but has a different emphasis: on feelings rather than content. The intent here is to identify and reflect the underlying feelings that you hear expressed in a person's statements. Although this may, at first, seem like an easy thing to do, it is among the most complex and difficult tasks that counselors undertake. To reflect feelings sensitively, accurately, and helpfully, you must be able to do the following:

1. Listen very carefully to subtle nuances of what is being said

2. Decode the deeper meanings of communication

3. Identify accurately the feelings a person is experiencing

4. Communicate this understanding in a way that can be accepted

Putting this skill of reflecting feelings into action would look and sound something like this:

Student: *"My friends think I should talk to you."*

Teacher: *"You're feeling pressured by your friends, but a part of you needs to talk about something bothering you."* [Note that the first part reflects the content, and the second part identifies the apprehension.]

Student: *"Yeah, I do need to talk about this, I guess."* (Silence)

Teacher: *"It's hard for you to do this."* (Even silence can be reflected.)

Student: (Deep breath) *"Here goes. My girlfriend wants to have sex, and I guess I do, too, but . . ."*

Teacher: *"You are supposed to want to have sex. You are the guy, but you also don't feel ready just yet."*

Student: *"Any guy would want to sleep with Karen. Me, too. My friends think I'm nuts. But I just think that sex should, well, you know . . ."*

Teacher: *"It's just more complicated for you than a simple act. You feel excited, apprehensive, and a little overwhelmed."*

And so continues a dialogue in which the teacher relies on reflection of feeling to help the adolescent explore his deeper feelings; clarify what he really wants; and, eventually, resolve what he wants to do—make his own decision—apart from pressures from his girlfriend, his friends, his family, and even the teacher. It is through such an exchange that it is possible for children to find out what they truly believe in and act on those convictions.

Practice Active Listening

Recruit the assistance of a classmate, friend, or colleague to help you practice active listening skills that include reflections of both content and feeling. Ask your partner to talk to you about something, anything, that he or she could go on about for a few minutes.

Listen *very* carefully to the underlying feelings being expressed beneath the content.

Take a stab at reflecting what you hear by using the stem, "You feel _____."

Naturally, this will feel somewhat awkward. Nevertheless, carry on your half of the conversation by continuing to respond with "you feel" statements.

The beauty of this technique is that it doesn't matter that much if you are on target or not. If you are inaccurate, the other person will simply tell you what is really being felt instead, as in the following:

You: *"So, you feel disappointed in yourself about that."*

Partner: *"Well, not so much disappointed as angry that I didn't get a fair chance."*

Self-Disclosure

This is the skill with which you demonstrate authenticity, genuineness, and humanness to students. Idealizing us as they sometimes do, it may be helpful for students to hear the ways that we have struggled with similar issues (if that is the case) and to connect with us on an intimate level.

Because this intervention has the potential for abuse (talking about yourself too much, too often, at inappropriate times, or revealing inappropriate material), self-disclosure should have certain features:

1. *It should be concise.* When you are talking about yourself, you have taken the focus off the other person you are trying to help.

2. *It should be devoid of self-indulgence.* Have a specific, defensible reason for what you are sharing, usually to highlight a specific point.

3. *It should be used very conservatively.* The danger is that by revealing too much about yourself, you will violate professional boundaries, reveal information about yourself that could be damaging, or focus too much on your own issues.

Self-disclosures are best employed when you wish to (a) demonstrate that the student is not alone, (b) bridge perceived distance between you, and (c) model openness.

Teacher: *"I know what you are going through. My parents were also divorced and I struggled for quite a while before I got my feet back on the ground."*

Another variety of self-disclosure, called *immediacy*, involves sharing what you are feeling about the interaction or what you are feeling toward the child at a particular moment in time:

Teacher: *"I really feel honored that you decided to trust me. I feel closer to you after what you've told me. And I respect you for your courage."*

Although we are talking about using self-disclosure in the context of a private, helping encounter, you have no doubt used this powerful technique in your classroom when you want to engage students on a personal level or provide an example from your own life to illustrate a point.

Summarizing

The summary, which is used at least once at the end of any conversation but can be inserted any time a wrap-up is needed, ties together themes that were discussed and puts things in perspective. Ideally, the teacher can summarize after having asked the student to do so first: "So, what are you leaving with?" The teacher can then fill in the gaps.

Teacher: *"I agree that we have helped you clarify your beliefs about sex and some aspects of your relationship with Karen. In addition, however, we looked at your desire to think for yourself more often instead of simply following the lead of others. You said you wished to tell your friends to respect your wishes and stop trying to push you. And you want to sit down with Karen and tell her how you feel."*

A good summary logically provides a transition between the exploration phase of helping and the action strategies for making needed changes. In many cases, you won't be the one who continues this dialogue because a referral to a professional might be indicated. Nevertheless, you have already set things up in such a way that the student can get the most from counseling.

ACTION SKILLS

Your role as a teacher will limit the action strategies you can employ. This will be frustrating for you because the one thing you will want to do—and that all beginners try to do—is to jump in and fix the problem—or at least fix what you *think* is the problem. One of most humbling things about counseling over a long period of time is coming to realize that people are far more complex than you can ever imagine and that their initial problems may have little resemblance to core issues that are at the heart of ongoing life struggles. In other words, when students approach you with some difficulty, keep in mind that that may be the excuse they are using to make contact with you. It may take some time before you get to the real reason they consulted you in the first place.

Just to complicate matters further, sometimes what students present to you really *is* what is bothering them most. They may very well have a specific problem that they want help sorting out, and it might lend itself to a single, brief conversation in order to bring things to a satisfactory resolution.

Most often, your helping role will be to listen, understand, and communicate empathy as you're helping the child clarify what the issues are. Then, you will refer the child for appropriate professional help.

As we mentioned, at times you will have the opportunity to help the child convert what has been discussed into some constructive action. The following skills are thus described to you with a note of caution: Get more training and supervision before you attempt any intrusive means of intervention. That especially includes giving advice, the single most abused helping strategy.

Checklist of Exploration Skills

Before You Begin	Clear your mind
	Resist distractions
	Stay neutral
	Focus concentration
	Take a deep breath
Positioning	Face the person fully
	Lean forward and attend
	Maintain relaxed eye contact
	Show expressive gestures
Observing	Observe carefully
	Listen intently
	Use your intuition and senses
Passive Listening	Animate yourself
	Maintain tranquility
	Smile appropriately
	Nod your head
	Use "uh-huhs"
Being With	Demonstrate empathy
	Communicate caring
	Feel compassion
	Show respect
	Reveal unconditional regard
	Be authentic
Responding	Ask open-ended questions
	Reflect content
	Reflect feelings
	Use self-disclosures appropriately
	Summarize as needed

Advice Giving

Don't do it. Period. Resist your natural inclination to tell people what to do with their lives. Are you sure you know what is best for anyone else? Do you really know what is best for *you?* Are you sure you want the responsibility that comes with telling someone else what to do?

Giving advice is most often done to make the teacher feel better rather than because it is actually helpful to the student. When someone comes to you in the depths of despair, you also feel powerless and helpless. You want to do something to make the pain go away. You want to bring instant relief. All you can think of is to tell the student something that you hope might be useful.

When you give advice, there are two possible outcomes, both of which are pretty bad. The first is that you give advice that turns out to be disastrous, in which case you will be blamed forever. It is *your* fault that you ruined this student's life.

The only thing worse than giving bad advice is giving *good* advice. Yes, you heard us correctly. Think about why providing sound guidance might actually be not at all a good thing.

When you tell someone what to do with his or her life, and it works out well, you've just taught this person to come back to you (or someone like you) in the future. You've also reinforced the idea that the person is too stupid to figure things out for himself or herself.

Certainly it is more time consuming and more laborious to help students figure out what they need to do for themselves. Ultimately, however, people are far more committed to actually following through on tasks if they came up with them on their own.

Student: *"So, what do you think I should do about this?"*

Teacher: *"What do* you *think you should do?"*

Student: *"I'm not sure. I was hoping you could tell me."*

Teacher: *"Well, let's see if you can come up with something and I'll help you put it into action. You said you had trouble making friends. I wonder what you could do to work on that."*

Student: *"You mean like go to one of those stupid meetings after school? You know I hate that. I already told you . . ."*

Teacher: *"Yes, that's one possibility, but I wonder what some other things are that you might try?"*

The teacher already had in mind what she actually wanted the student to do, that is, to get more involved in afterschool activities as a way to meet other kids and make more friends, but she wanted the student to come up with this on his own. If she just told him to go try out for a play, or play intramural sports, or join the chess club, or whatever, it is highly unlikely he would actually do it.

The exceptions to this prohibition of giving advice take place only when children are tempted to do something that is potentially dangerous to themselves or others. Imagine, for example, that a student tells you that she is going to go out with a bunch of guys who are known for taking advantage of other girls, or a student tells you that he is going to stand up to his drunken father, or someone else thinks she needs to lose more weight and she is already way too thin. Under such circumstances, you are not only permitted but *required* to do something. Remember, however, that the way you offer advice will determine the extent to which a child is likely to pay attention to and follow your words of wisdom.

Teacher: *"I think that before you take such a drastic step, you should talk to some people. Tell your friends, only the ones you trust, what you have in mind. Hear what they have to say. Then let's talk again."*

Goal Setting

This is the consummate action skill, the one that satisfies both your and your student's need to translate some elusive, ambiguous issue into concrete results. Unlike dreaded homework assignments, however, this kind of goal is definitely not prescribed by you—many children already may feel resentment toward teachers for telling them what to do. Instead, you will take the longer, more laborious route of helping children define and follow through on their own stated goals; that way, they are much more likely to complete them. Even if they don't do what they said they would, you can unconcernedly shrug and say, "Oh, well, I guess you didn't want to do it after all." Then, when the student replies, "But I did! I did want to do it. I just didn't have time," you can smile and reply, "Fine. You'll do it when you want."

There are other factors to keep in mind when helping people set goals for themselves:

1. *Make sure the goal that they identify is really related to the central issue with which they are struggling.* Losing 10 pounds may be a very good thing to do, but if one's weight isn't the major impediment to high self-esteem, then efforts could be wasted.

2. *Construct goals that are realistic and attainable.* A student enthusiastic to change can become overzealous, naively believing he or she can do everything overnight. Help students take small, manageable steps, ensuring that they will experience success in their efforts. A child who has few friends, for example, could start with carrying on two-minute conversations with others before undertaking progressively more difficult tasks.

3. *Whenever possible, make the goals as specific as possible.* Include what the person will do, where he or she will do it, when and how often it will be done, for how long it will be continued, with whom, who will be present, and what contingencies will be in place if he or she should falter. These factors can help translate a student's imprecise concerns into action goals. For example,

> Before: *"I get in fights a lot. I want to stop but other kids sometimes push me too far. I let them do that. I also know that I can't keep fighting all the time or I won't have any friends left. No teeth either. So, I guess what I have to do is stop fighting so much."*

> After: *"Between now and tomorrow at this time, I will not get in a single physical fight with anyone at school. (I can't guarantee what might happen at home with my brothers.) If I should start to lose my temper during the next day at school, I will repeat to myself what we've talked about. If that doesn't work too well, I give you my word, no, I mean I promise to myself that I will walk away. If I absolutely have to defend myself, I will do so only with my mouth, not my fists."*

As can be seen, this young man's goal for the next 24 hours meets the criteria described earlier. Sometimes, you can make a tremendous difference in a person's life by having him or her talk things out and decide what to do, and then helping him or her create a plan to get what he or she wants.

You can experiment with this strategy in your own life by thinking of some behavior you'd like to change. The more specific you can be, the better. Write a contract stating what you will do, when you will do it, and where and with whom this will take place. Remember to be realistic, that is, to declare something that you know you can do within the declared time parameters.

Problem Solving

A more elaborate version of goal setting, involving a sequential series of steps, is applying a problem-solving approach to a student's difficulties. Assume, for example, that a student wants to go to college but doesn't have the financial means or an academic track record that would qualify her for a scholarship. The student feels frustrated and hopeless, ready to give up the dream and resolve herself to menial, repetitive work. Without solving the problem for the student, or telling the student what you think she should do, you can still introduce a systematic way of attacking the challenge, one that will be useful in many other similar situations in life.

"Okay," the teacher might begin, "let's come up with a plan together. Why don't we write down on paper a specific program for how you might find some possible funding sources and then narrow down those to the ones that have the best chance for success?"

Any problem-solving strategy would have the following components:

1. Define the problem

2. Specify the goals

3. Develop alternatives that might be constructive

4. Narrow the choices to those that seem most realistic

5. Put the plan into action

With the help of her teacher, the student generated a surprisingly long list of possibilities, ranging from going to summer school, hiring a tutor, finding a better-paying job, going to a community college, working for a while after graduation to save money before going to college, contacting civic organizations that sponsor needy students, or joining the military to earn college tuition. After limiting the choices to the few that seemed most appealing, the student was able to target her energy on a specific plan that was quite within her reach.

Reframing

Imagine a nice picture in an ugly frame, one that so detracts from the art that it loses its luster and appeal. Take the same picture, put it in a different frame, and voila!—a true thing of beauty! That is an analogy for reframing in a helping context.

A most creative, challenging, and fun endeavor, reframing is a skill that takes some time to learn. It is a way of thinking about things that people present to you in a completely different light. Your task is to take a problem that someone describes, usually one about which you can do little, and then reframe it in such a way that solutions more readily suggest themselves. In its most basic mode, you take what the student has said—"I'm stupid" (a predicament that, if it were true, you could do little to help)—and then alter it so that it appears more easily resolvable: "You are less talented than you would like to be in quantitative subjects, but you are quite brilliant at drawing funny pictures and fixing things that are broken. That doesn't sound like someone who is stupid to me."

Here are some other examples of reframing in action:

Statement	Reframing
"I'm shy."	*"You act shyly when you are in new situations without your close friends around."*
"I hate school."	*"You don't enjoy structured learning very much, but you really do like school when you have freedom to do what you want."*
"My child says that all of his teachers say he is disruptive. My child is not disruptive."	*"Your child has a great sense of humor. He is just performing for the wrong audience."*
"Your lectures are boring."	*"You find it hard to concentrate on content presentations."*

In each case, the teacher seeks to reframe the definition of the problem in a more optimistic light. Sometimes this works; sometimes it doesn't. As with all helping efforts, we try a variety of approaches until we find the right combination. The main idea behind this intervention is that you change the way the initial problem is defined by the student so that it is far more likely that some success can be attained. Certainly you'd agree that telling yourself, "I'm terrible at this counseling stuff and I'll never get it," is a pretty discouraging statement about a problem. Compare it with the alternative: "Like any new skills, it will take me some time and practice before I feel comfortable using them fluently."

Cognitive Restructuring

Reframing is a cognitive intervention that helps people shift the way they view their concerns (as in the previous example). Other techniques help children think differently about their plights; the most popular of these techniques are known as *cognitive therapy.*

The theory behind these techniques is quite simple: What we feel is based on how we think about what is happening. If we change the way we interpret a predicament, we can thus change how we feel about it. Our job, then, is to teach children to realize that they have choices about how they can react to events in their lives. Very little is intrinsically bad or annoying or frustrating. It is our perception of these experiences that determines our reactions. "If you don't like how you are feeling," the cognitive therapist says, "then change how you think about it!"

This approach to helping should be exciting to you for a number of reasons. First, it is easily learned, and with a little practice, you will find yourself becoming more and more skilled at helping people understand that the way they think about their problems determines, to a great extent, how they subsequently feel and behave. Second, this is a problem-solving approach that you can apply immediately to your own life. In fact, the more you work on your own internal thinking patterns, the more proficient you will be in helping others with theirs. Likewise, the more you practice helping children confront their irrational beliefs and illogical thoughts, the more you will notice profound changes in your own personal effectiveness. Third, and most exciting of all, using these cognitive strategies can make a difference in a student's life in a very short period of time.

The process of cognitive helping follows a fairly logical sequence in which you first help a student articulate the feelings that are bothersome. The helping skills mentioned earlier (active listening, reflections of feeling, open-ended questioning) are often useful.

Teacher: *"What exactly are you feeling right now?"*

Student: *"I don't know. Just kind of upset."*

Teacher: *"You're feeling down about something."*

Student: *"Yes, I'm down all right. But I'm also really angry!"*

Teacher: *"I can see that. You sure seem angry. But also hurt."*

So far, the teacher has helped the student identify four different feelings she is experiencing—upset, down, angry, and hurt. With more time, the list could be lengthened even further because we usually feel many different things when we are upset about something.

Another step that you can take at this stage is to ask the student to rate on a 1-to-10 scale the intensity of feeling for each of the identified emotions. For example, if she is feeling extremely angry, she might rate that an 8 or 9, but if she is feeling only moderately down, then she would rate that a 5. Because it is unrealistic to eliminate all emotional reactions to disturbing situations, this allows you to create a baseline from which to measure the effects of your help afterwards.

Next, the student would be encouraged to describe the particular situation that she believes is causing her the problems. At this juncture, the student describes exactly what took place.

Teacher: *"Tell me what happened."*

Student: *"Oh, you know, that dumb play I tried out for."*

Teacher: *"You didn't do as well as you hoped, huh?"*

Student: *"You can say that again. I didn't even get called back for another reading."*

So, the incident that the student feels has "ruined her life forever" is not getting a part in a play.

Because the point of this helping procedure is that other people or events don't make you feel anything—you make yourself feel things based on how you think—the next step is to help the student identify the internal thoughts or irrational beliefs that are creating the suffering. This part is a bit tricky because it requires you to be familiar with the main themes prevalent in irrational thinking. Basically, irrational beliefs fall into three main groups:

1. *Exaggerations of reality.* People make things seem much worse than they really are by distorting the significance of what took place: "Because I didn't get the part in the play, I'll never do what I want in life." Or, "Everyone will laugh at me when they find out." Clearly, these are gross exaggerations, because in the first case, the student is overgeneralizing, and in the second instance, there is little evidence that that is true.

2. *Demands that the world be different.* This set of irrational beliefs results from expectations that the world or people be different from the way they are. We set ourselves up as special beings who deserve special attention. Common manifestations of this irrational thinking usually begin with the pronouncement, "It's not fair . . . that I didn't get what I want . . . that he treated me that way . . . that the rules were changed." This thinking is irrational because, clearly, the world is not fair. We are not entitled to special attention (even though we may want it). And just because we have certain expectations for people, it does not mean that they are obligated to live up to them.

3. *Judging oneself in absolute terms.* This is a variation of the previous irrational thinking in which the student applies unrealistic or perfectionist standards to himself or herself that he or she could never live up to. For example:

"Because I didn't perform as well as I would like in this situation, I will never be good at this, or anything."

"Because I got a D on this exam, I am stupid."

"Because she won't go out with me, I'll never meet anyone I like who likes me back."

Words like *must*, *should*, and *never* are clues that we are making demands of ourselves that are self-imposed and probably not realistic.

Even with just a thumbnail sketch of irrational themes, you have some idea of how the teacher could move the child to the last and most important stage—challenging those irrational beliefs and confronting their veracity. These interventions require that you be able to apply cognitive techniques to yourself before you can work successfully with others. In other words, you can't talk people into letting go of their dysfunctional thinking unless you can dispute your own.

In the case we have been following, the dialogue might develop as follows:

Teacher: *"So what you are saying is that because you didn't get this part in the play, you are a worthless person?"*

Student: *"Yup."* (Nods head in agreement)

Teacher: *"And that makes sense to you? Because this one time you weren't chosen for a part, therefore you are a completely, totally terrible actor, not to mention a worthless person?"*

Student: *"But I wanted to be in the play so badly."*

Teacher: *"I understand that. But what makes little sense is that you are saying that because you wanted something very badly, and didn't get it this one time, it means that everything you did before doesn't matter, and everything you will do in the future is ruined."*

Student: *"Okay, so maybe I exaggerated a little. But you have to agree that the whole audition was a crock."*

Teacher: *"Let's assume that you are right: It wasn't fair. So what?"*

Student: *"Huh?"*

Teacher: *"Since when are auditions fair and impartial?"*

Student: *"But they should be fair! I mean . . ."*

Teacher: *"That's not the point. I agree with you. And after this, let's talk about what you could do to change the system. But for now, why are you so surprised that the selection process isn't fair? This isn't the first time you have encountered favoritism in the selection process."*

Student: (Nods in agreement.)

Teacher: *"Look, you can't change what happened, but you can change the way you think about it. The only thing worse than not getting the part is not getting the part and then making yourself miserable for days afterwards."*

This interaction gives you a flavor of the rich opportunities available to teach students to feel more control over their internal states. Children feel so little power in their lives that it is especially exciting to introduce them to a way of thinking that allows them to decide how they want to feel about things.

The student who was upset about not getting the part in the play left the encounter with her teacher still a bit upset about the situation, but not nearly as much as before.

The map of cognitive interventions highlights the strategy in which students are challenged to do the following:

1. Accept greater responsibility for their thoughts and feelings

2. Be more aware of what is going on inside their heads

3. Become more analytical and logical in the ways they reason through cause-effect relationships

4. Make choices about how they want to react to the things and people around them

5. Change the ways they feel by altering the ways they think

The teacher closes her talk with the student by reinforcing these very ideas:

It is no wonder that you were upset. It wasn't only a matter of not getting the part, but also the way you reacted to that situation. It is understandable that you would be disappointed, but not so down that you can barely function—that, you did to yourself. Any time in the future that you don't like the way you are feeling, you can follow this same procedure to figure out what you are saying to yourself about the event, and then to change your internal thoughts.

The object of these confrontations is to help students realize the extent of their distortions and substitute more realistic and appropriate responses. Confrontations come in other forms as well.

The whole process through which we just went is reviewed in the chart on page 70.

Although the student wasn't able to eliminate all of her negative feelings in a single conversation with her teacher, she was able to make rather significant progress in a short time. Best of all, she can apply this method any time she likes with any other problem or disappointment that comes up.

Confront Irrational Beliefs

The best way to learn this cognitive strategy is to apply it to yourself. Start by picking a situation in your life that you feel a little upset about. (It's better to start with something small.)

It is this last step of challenging irrational internal thoughts that requires the most practice and persistence. It is worthwhile to consult a few of the recommended readings that provide more detail about this helping system. The key to being able to use it effectively with others is first to be able to apply it to yourself. The next time you catch yourself upset about something that is not going the way you expected or hoped,

Map of Cognitive Interventions

A	B
Activating Event	**Irrational Beliefs**
"I didn't get the part in the play."	• *"This isn't fair!"* • *"I'll never get what I want."* • *"Everyone will laugh."* • *"This is the worst thing that could happen."*

C	D
Emotional Consequences	**Disputing Irrational Beliefs**
1–10 Scale	
• Upset 9 • Depressed 5 • Hurt 8 • Anger 9 • Shame 7	• *"True, life isn't fair. So what?"* • *"Just because I didn't get this part doesn't mean I'm not a good person, or even a good actor."* • *"Some people might laugh, but not the ones I care about."* • *"This isn't awful, only a minor setback."*

E

New Emotional Effect

New Rating 1–10	
• Upset 5 • Depressed 2 • Hurt 2 • Anger 6 • Shame 1	• *"Well, I can't just drop this completely."* • *"I don't feel so bad anymore."* • *"I understand this wasn't personal."* • *"I'm still pretty angry."* • *"Nobody really cares but me."*

try examining what you are telling yourself about this situation that may be making things far worse. Once you catch yourself exaggerating, distorting, awfulizing, or otherwise thinking irrationally, try substituting more appropriate, reasonable, thoughtful reactions as an alternative.

Strategic Interventions

One of the most practical developments in the counseling field involves the use of rather brief, focused interventions that are designed to break long-standing dysfunctional patterns. Although it is beyond the scope and training of a teacher to use some of these strategies (they are very potent and need to be practiced under supervision), you may find it interesting to learn about some of the action techniques that are now available. In some cases, you might consult with a school counselor or psychologist to employ these methods.

1. Describe the incident. _____
   _____
   _____

2. List the emotional reactions you feel. Next to each one, rate on a 1-to-10
   scale how intense the feelings are (under the "1st Rating").

Emotion	1st Rating	2nd Rating
_____	_____	_____
_____	_____	_____
_____	_____	_____
_____	_____	_____
_____	_____	_____

3. Write out the irrational beliefs inside your head that are creating the
   emotional suffering. Look for themes related to the following:

   a. Use of *shoulds* or *musts* in which you demand that the world or other
      people be a certain way
   b. Exaggerations of reality in which you "awfulize" the situation
   c. Whining about things not being fair
   d. Judging yourself absolutely based on isolated behavior
   e. Telling yourself you can't stand what happened even though it is only
      disappointing or annoying

Identified Irrational Beliefs

_____
_____
_____
_____
_____
_____

1. Dispute each of those beliefs by asking yourself these questions:

   ♦ Where is the evidence this is so?
   ♦ Where is it written that this is the way it must be?
   ♦ How am I exaggerating what is happening?
   ♦ Is this really terrible, or only annoying?

2. After completing these steps, go back and rate your original emotional
   reactions again, noting changes you have been able to make.

Paradoxical Directive

This is a fancy term for describing "reverse psychology," or asking someone to do the opposite of what is desired. A student who worries excessively to the point that he cannot sleep at night may be asked to deliberately stay awake as long as possible, jotting in a journal every hour that he is still not sleeping. The intention is to stop the worrying about worrying; that is, remaining awake is no longer a problem but is now the assigned task.

Prescribing the Symptom

For example, a student who continually disrupts class and who has resisted every effort to curtail his behavior might be asked to deliberately disrupt class as an exercise. Sometimes, it takes the fun out of even rebellious behavior when you're ordered to do it.

Miracle Question

When a student feels stuck and hopeless, you can ask her to imagine a time in the future when the problem has been resolved. Then, the student can be asked how this miracle occurred. This is an indirect way to get someone to supply a solution to her own problem.

Identify Exceptions

When a student describes himself in absolute terms, as in, "I have a problem with numbers," or "I'm not good at talking in front of other people," or "I've always been this way," you ask for exceptions to the rule. "Think of a time," you might say, "in which you were able to do well in this area." Because you will often get a shrug as a response, it is necessary to dig deeply in order to find an exception. The main goal of this strategy is to help the student realize the extent to which he is exaggerating the problem and overgeneralizing its effects: Rarely does someone exhibit problematic behavior in all circumstances. The intention is focus on the exceptions.

Externalizing

The opposite of helping students become responsible for their behavior is to help them disown self-blame. This involves speaking about the problem as if it is external to the student: "So, when you feel this urge to start a fight, when does it come upon you?" This switch in language sometimes makes it easier to talk about an issue without the student feeling attacked or defensive. It also makes the student and teacher allies working together to defeat "the enemy."

Power Hierarchies

Individual behavior rarely occurs in isolation; it is often a response to what other people are doing. This circular causality means that in order to change one student's behavior, you might have to look at how it is being reinforced, encouraged, or stimulated by others in your class, your own actions, or the family. Interventions can thus take the form of making changes in the way power is allocated. For instance, you could schedule a parent conference in which you empower the student by putting her in charge of the meeting.

The list above is but a sampling of the brief therapy strategies that are available for prompting sometimes rather dramatic changes in behavior. You may find it useful to seek out a counselor or therapist who has training in this area and ask her to consult with you about difficult situations that you can't resolve on your own.

Confrontation

There are times when people need to hear that they have crossed a boundary or when they need to understand the discrepancies between what they are doing and what they said they want, or what they are saying now versus what they said earlier. The secret is to confront someone in such a way that he or she will not feel defensive.

The best confrontations are thus presented neutrally, matter-of-factly, even tentatively, as if to say that you have noticed something interesting that the person might find helpful: Gee, I'm confused. You're saying that you want good grades in school, yet you mentioned earlier that you never study.

You are putting the observation before students and letting them decide what they want to do about it. Obviously, this is the most intrusive of interventions and, hence, the one that must be applied most cautiously and carefully. You can as easily alienate or wound someone deeply with a mistimed or insensitive confrontation as you can help facilitate a major breakthrough. Therefore, before attempting any confrontation, the key is to ask yourself whether you are offering this intervention out of caring for the other person or whether it represents an attempt to be punitive or to put the person down.

In the following example, the teacher tries to confront a student but with a style that sparks defensiveness:

Teacher: *"I don't think you're stupid at all. On the contrary, you just don't seem to put much effort into things."*

Student: *"Wait a minute. Are you saying I'm lazy? 'Cause if you are, I resent that!"*

In this case, the student felt defensive and attacked even though the teacher was only trying to be helpful. So, the conversation is easily side-tracked into an avenue that is a dead end. However, if the confrontation is worded differently, the outcome can be quite different as well.

Teacher: *"I've heard you say so many times about how stupid you are. I'm not sure what you mean by that. Surely you can think of instances in which you've been really smart."*

Student: *"Yeah. Yeah. You're right. I am pretty good at figuring out how stories will end. My friends get mad at me because I always guess the endings of movies."*

In this second example, the teacher is careful to confront the student by inviting her to look at exceptions to the self-claim that she is stupid. The teacher does not get in the student's face as much as neutrally point out a discrepancy that has been observed. Thus, the best confrontations are those in which people don't know they are being confronted.

Encouragement

We saved the best for last. Students experience certain concerns for which there are no easy solutions and about which you can do little except offer support. Encouragement is listed here as an action skill because it is a deliberate and intentional effort on your part to foster hope in those who are without it.

Imagine a child who finds out she has leukemia, or another whose father died in a hunting accident, or still another whose parents are separating, or one who just found out she will be moving out of state. What would you propose to do in these situations? The answer, of course, is that your act of doing is really one of encouragement.

You communicate, in effect, that you have complete confidence that the child will indeed recover a positive state of mind. Furthermore, you intend to be there for him or her along the way. Because you believe in the child's power and strength, he or she will regain a sense of balance. Sometimes, your support is all you have to give.

SUGGESTED ACTIVITIES

1. Find a partner to work with and practice the skills mentioned in this chapter. Start with basic attending skills:
   a. Carry on a conversation with your partner in which neither of you maintains eye contact; then, after a few minutes, concentrate on making good eye contact. Notice the difference.

b. Continue your conversation but with both of you showing blank expressions on your faces; after a few minutes, both of you show animation, warmth, and expressiveness in your face. Notice the difference.

c. As you continue your talk, add to these attending skills a more concerted effort on your part to use head nods, "uh-huhs," and other acknowledgments that you are following and understanding what your partner is saying. Notice the effect.

2. Choose a partner with whom to work. One of you should be the "client" first, and the other the "helper." The client should play the role of a child who feels left out of activities during recess and wants to stay inside with the teacher. The helper should respond only with active listening skills, primarily restatements and reflections of feeling.

3. With a partner, you can practice asking open-ended questions that encourage rather than cut off communication. Each of you should write down three questions that you believe will elicit maximum information from your partner and encourage him or her to examine important issues. Ask your questions of one another and note their effectiveness.

4. Concentrate on a few of the skills presented in this chapter and make them part of the normal way you relate to others. Find opportunities every day to practice your new skills. Report to your peers the ways in which you are aware that there are differences in your interpersonal style.

5. Recruit the assistance of an expert who can observe you applying the skills in this chapter (or record an interview on tape). Ask for specific feedback on ways you could improve your performance.

SUGGESTED READING

Egan, G. (2006). *The skilled helper: A problem management and opportunity development approach to helping* (8th ed.). Belmont, CA: Wadsworth.

Evans, D. R., Hearn, M. T., Uhlemann, M. R., & Ivey, A. E. (2004). *Essential interviewing: A programmed approach to effective communication* (6th ed.). Belmont, CA: Wadsworth.

Hazler, R. J. (1998). *Helping in the hallways: Advanced strategies for enhancing school relationships.* Thousand Oaks, CA: Corwin Press.

Kottler, J. A., & Carlson, J. (2002). *Bad therapy: Master therapists share their worst failures.* New York: Brunner/Routledge.

Kottler, J. A., & Carlson, J. (2003). *The mummy at the dining room table: Eminent therapists reveal their most unusual cases and what they teach us about human behavior.* San Francisco: Jossey-Bass.

Kottler, J. A., & Carlson, J. (2006). *The client who changed me: Stories of therapist personal transformation.* New York: Brunner/Routledge.

Murphy, J. J. (2005). *Solution-focused counseling in middle and high schools.* Upper Saddle River, NJ: Prentice Hall.

Sklare, G. (2004). *Brief counseling that works: A solution-focused approach for school counselors and administrators* (2nd ed). Thousand Oaks, CA: Corwin Press.

Ungar, M. (2006). *Strengths-based counseling with at-risk youth.* Thousand Oaks, CA: Corwin Press.

Wilson, R., & Branch. R. (2006). *Cognitive behavioral therapy for dummies.* New York: John Wiley.

Wright, J. H., Basco, M. R., & Thase M. E. (2005). *Learning cognitive behavioral therapy: An illustrated guide.* Arlington VA: American Psychiatric Press.

Counseling Skills in the Classroom $\quad$ **5**

A lthough thus far we have been discussing the use of counseling skills in the context of private conversations with troubled students, every one of the techniques previously mentioned can also be used in group and classroom contexts. In one of many examples we will present, notice the way a teacher responds to a student disruption in class:

Student: *"I don't see the point of what we're doing. Can I go to the toilet? I gotta go bad."* (Other students laugh)

Teacher: *"You're bored with what we're doing right now and wish we could do something else more interesting to you."*

Rather than choosing the most obvious responses, such as scolding the student, answering the concrete question, or just ignoring the disruption, the teacher reflects back what he hears. Although initially he was feeling annoyed and threatened by the interruption, he quickly "reframed" the comment as helpful in giving him feedback.

There are many other ways you can use counseling skills in the classroom in addition to reflecting the content and feelings of what students say. You can concentrate on using open rather than closed questions to promote more exploration. You can summarize discussions at various points to make connections and bring together diverse contributions. Probably most significant, you can attend to the emotional aspects of student experience as well as nourish their brains. This helps to build a learning community emphasizing values of curiosity, respect, tolerance, responsibility, and caring. After all, students can (and do) learn as much from one another as they do from their teachers.

DEVELOPING COMMUNITIES OF
RESPECT AND TOLERANCE

It is through building communities of respect and tolerance that teachers help students feel more comfortable in the classroom, regardless of their unique characteristics. This process begins when teachers allow time in class to discuss topics of greatest relevance, regardless of what is on the lesson plan. For instance, a third-grade class was invited to put aside their math assignments for the hour and instead to talk about the public demonstrations in the community on immigration reform. In an eleventh-grade economics class, the teacher postponed the theory of Max Weber to devote some time talking about a new school policy that upset many of the students. A seventh-grade health class became sidetracked from the topic of sexually transmitted diseases when it was disclosed that one of the student's older siblings died recently of a drug overdose. In each of these cases, the teacher employed counseling skills to respond to pressing student needs, later returning to the assigned lesson (and working hard to catch up).

Whether topics range from a recent incidence of school violence to a provocative television show or music video, the teacher acts as facilitator to help students give voice to their thoughts and feelings in a respectful and constructive way. Since every class and group has participants who talk too much, and others who don't talk much at all, the teacher's role is to make sure that everyone is heard and understood. This can be done by setting a one-minute rule for contributions, by allowing each person to speak only once, by going around the room in a circle in which everyone checks in, or by inviting comments only from quieter class members. Students can even be "deputized" as coleaders of the discussion to get them more involved in taking responsibility for their own learning.

Settling Conflicts and Disputes

There are times when students act out in class, engage in abusive or disrespectful behavior, or otherwise disrupt what is going on. From what you have learned previously, you would first assess the situation and the context of the student's behavior.

- What is the *meaning* of this action?
- What are the *benefits* or "secondary gains" the student is enjoying as a result? Attention? Control? Entertainment?
- What are the *consequences* of the behavior, for better or worse?
- What do you notice that *you* are feeling inside, some of which has more to do with you than with the student?
- What is the *context* of what is going on, based on what is happening in the child's life or in the classroom?

- What evidence do you see for *psychological problems* that may be operating? Depression? Anxiety? Abuse? Neglect? Substance abuse?

Even if you can't immediately diagnose what the student is really communicating by the behavior (which is most often the case), this process still slows you down so you don't take things so personally. It gives you time to take a deep breath and reflect on the situation before you respond impulsively and perhaps escalate the conflict.

It is your job to protect student welfare; this is perhaps even more important than any teaching you do. Just as physicians are admonished to do no harm, so too are teachers serving the role of providing safety for children who might otherwise be living in adversarial, or even abusive, environments. That is why you *must* intervene if you observe (or even sense) that students are harassing others, especially based on their culture, race, religion, sexual orientation, or physical/mental challenges.

Many such conflicts can be avoided if you are able to use counseling skills to create an atmosphere in your classes in which everyone is responsible for the welfare of others. Instead of waiting for disruptive or abusive incidents to occur, you can build this kind of caring community from the outset.

Confronting Bullying and Harassment

We have seen the consequences of ignoring incidents of bullying and harassment, not just in terms of enduring damage to the victims, but also the ways that such individuals may respond with dramatic violence of their own. You would only need to consult your own history in school to recall one or more incidents in which you felt terrorized, teased, or humiliated by others (sometimes even a teacher). Such experiences remain painful and haunting throughout a lifetime.

You see examples of harassment or abuse in the school, if not in your own classroom. Other incidents will be reported to you by others who are either victims of bullying or who themselves have witnessed such actions. Most such behaviors continue because they are tolerated instead of challenged.

Classroom discussions can help students become more mindful of bullying and harassment. You can discuss the consequences experienced by the bully, the victim, and any bystanders. Such conversations often lead to very intense feelings being expressed, particularly since there is a high probability that some victims in your class have never been able to talk freely about what they've suffered.

This leads to further discussion about the most appropriate ways to respond to bullies, or to observed incidents of racism, prejudice, or harassment. In one school, this had become such a priority that when a new student started to bother a classmate, other students immediately intervened, explaining: "We don't do that here."

Modeling Genuine Care and Concern

Students want to see that their teachers care about them. They want teachers to be in charge, set limits, and promote mutual respect for individuals. Students also want to be seen as individuals.

Teachers who demonstrate caring do so by structuring classes in ways that are meaningful and that make learning relevant and motivating. They get to know their students on an individual basis. They are responsive to what interests student, as well as sensitive to what bothers them. They "check in" to see what is happening in their lives, their accomplishments, their challenges. This can easily be done by standing at the door and greeting students as they enter and/or making time while students are working on their own to chat with them one at a time. You can find out more about your students by developing a survey for them to complete and/or responding to journal prompts. Another way is to observe students outside the classroom during extracurricular activities. Students love to see their teachers sitting in the stands of the athletic field or in a theater audience.

We caution teachers to be sensitive in responding to and involving all children in the classroom. Students like teachers who are fair, firm, and consistent. Teachers need to be careful not to exhibit favoritism. Unconsciously they may show preference to a particular child or children. Monitoring interactions so as to ensure equity is extremely important. Smile and make eye contact with all children. Give them plenty of time to reflect on a statement or question before responding. Use a system for keeping track of who you call on. You may want to use a list of names or a seating chart. That way you can be sure that you treating all students equitably.

Setting High Expectations and Praising Accomplishments

High expectations show students that you have faith in their ability and will support them. They need to know you believe they can be successful, and you should tell them so. Let your optimism shine. As you call on students, be sure to give them plenty of time to frame their responses. Help by giving them hints or clues. As you monitor student behavior by scanning the room or walking around, continually encourage their efforts with smiles and comments.

Praise students' accomplishments when it is deserved. Specific praise for work done well is motivating. Use "I" messages to tell them how proud you are. Congratulate them on their successes. Help them to acknowledge their progress. Depending on their age and cultures, you may want to do this privately rather than publicly. You can write notes to students and/or send notes home.

Just as you would do during private conversations, use reflecting and summarizing skills to let students know that you are tracking and understanding what they are saying.

HELPING STRATEGIES IN GROUPS

We began this chapter by stressing that you can apply the skills of helping in settings other than individual conferences. Although there is no substitute for the intimacy and focused attention of being with a child in private, it is often impractical to find both the time and opportunity to do so in light of everything else that infringes on your time—papers to grade, lessons to prepare, meetings to attend—already more than you can handle comfortably. Working with children in groups is an alternative way to help many children deal with troublesome issues, especially if you can adjust the usual ways you run your classroom.

DIFFERENCES BETWEEN PROCESS AND CLASSROOM GROUPS

Most of your training in group leadership was designed to help you present information and assess the degree to which children learned this material. Thus, you are prepared to give lectures, use audiovisual aids in your presentations, devise projects for students to work on in groups, divide the class into study groups for cooperative learning, and play team games with children.

In contrast, process-oriented groups provide different kinds of educational experiences for students. There are several ways that teachers commonly focus on process. If you start a class at the beginning of the school year by having the students develop their own conduct rules, then you are exposing them to a particular method you want them to learn. If you focus classroom discussion on how students feel about a topic, then you are working in a process-oriented way. The same is true if you conduct some sort of simulation game and then debrief students afterwards. If a provocative or controversial issue arises in class, and you encourage students to share their opinions on the matter and then help them toward some sort of resolution, it is clear that the process of what unfolds is just as important as the content of the discussion.

Specifically, these growth-oriented experiences differ from the usual classroom instruction in the following ways:

• *The emphasis is not on content.* There is no specific information that you wish students to learn in process groups. Your intent, instead, is to provide a safe environment in which children may explore their own values, feelings, and beliefs about themselves, others, and their experiences.

• *Participants are encouraged to share their own personal reactions to ideas rather than ideas themselves.* Unlike the usual classroom activities that focus on intellectual ideas or the development of skills, process groups require participants to speak about their very personal reactions to what they have experienced and are experiencing.

• *Small talk, rambling, and focus on outsiders is not permitted.* It is crucial to keep attention on what is taking place in the group. You do not let children complain about what others are doing, nor do you let them ramble, intellectualize, or engage in meaningless prattle; you keep them focused on what they are feeling and thinking. You make sure that time is equitably distributed among all children.

• *Process groups are student centered rather than teacher centered.* In many classroom arrangements, the teacher stands before the class presenting content. All eyes and ears in the room are supposed to be attending to this one person, clearly the most important person in the room. It is rare, for example, that students take notes on what other students say. In process groups, however, the teacher plays a supportive role; it is the children who do most of the talking and who are clearly the ones whose contributions are most important. The leader's role is not to instruct but rather to guide the process.

• *Children speak only for themselves.* The pronoun *I* is emphasized over *we* or *you.* The object is to help students express themselves more honestly, clarify their own beliefs, and respond to one another sensitively.

• *The teacher's attention is focused primarily on the dynamics and process of the group.* It is not so much what the children say as how they say it, and their relationship to one another, that draws the leader's attention. Who is getting along with whom? What coalitions have formed? What degree of cohesion has developed? What are the children avoiding dealing with? What is the meaning of any silence?

As should be clear from the preceding descriptions, process groups typically arise in two different ways. First, something spontaneously crops up in class that lends itself to in-depth processing. Perhaps there has been a tragedy in the community. Maybe one of the students in the class is having a problem with which others can relate. Even more common, you can sense beneath the surface some strong emotional overtones to what students are saying, showing, or trying to hide. Of course, you would not choose to focus on process in all instances; if you did, you would hardly have time for anything else. Furthermore, you will want to channel things in this direction only when you think it is constructive at that moment in time. Balance is the key.

The second type of process group that you would likely use is a deliberate structure that is part of your learning environment. Perhaps you will have students role-play a scene from literature or history and then have them talk about what was stirred up for them. You could put students in small groups and direct them to talk about something related to the current topic that they don't understand, and how they feel about that. You could schedule regular intervals each week in which students can talk about things that are bothering them, or perhaps just things they are wondering about. In all these cases, your job is to facilitate the interactions so that students talk to one another, respect different opinions, and learn to respond appropriately.

ADVANTAGES AND DISADVANTAGES OF PROCESS GROUPS

Process groups have a number of advantages over individual helping efforts. For example, a crisis in the community could reveal that a number of children have concerns about a similar issue (drugs, violence, disasters, and so on). Children have their feelings publicly validated and realize that they are not alone in having these feelings. In groups, you can obviously reach more children and make more efficient use of your time than in one-to-one conversations. Additionally, group structures provide a support system for change; teach children skills for succeeding in social situations; facilitate an atmosphere of intimacy and trust; and, most important, provide opportunities for constructive feedback from their peers. A number of teachers also report that introducing process group experiences into their classrooms makes their jobs more fun. They feel as if they are truly making a difference in children's lives when they can observe significant changes in the way the students think, feel, and behave in a relatively short period of time.

Process groups are not without their disadvantages, however. Because they can be such powerful educational and therapeutic modalities, they have the potential to do as much harm as good. Indeed, more than a few people have suffered emotional casualties in groups because the leader was untrained or unprepared to handle critical situations. Leading process groups thus requires more skills and a higher degree of leadership competence than do ordinary teaching responsibilities or even individual work with children. Peer pressure, forced conformity, less control, and increased complexity all contribute to a situation in which a teacher can quickly feel over his or her head if not adequately prepared.

These disadvantages and advantages are summarized in Table 5.1. If you wish to lead process group activities in your classes to facilitate children's emotional maturity, in addition to their academic achievement, you should keep several things in mind:

Table 5.1   Advantages and Disadvantages of Process Group Work

Advantages	Disadvantages
Uses resources more efficiently	Confidentiality difficult to enforce
Encourages intimacy and trust	Requires more skill and competence
Provides support system for change	Forces conformity and peer pressure
Teaches skills for interpersonal success	Students receive less individual help and attention
Provides opportunities for vicarious learning	Leader has less control and influence
Helps kids practice new behaviors	Casualties can occur, especially when leaders are untrained and students are pressured to do things for which they don't feel ready
Provides honest feedback	
Makes the teacher's job more fun	

1. Don't attempt any structure without supervision available from someone who has more training (such as a school counselor, social worker, or psychologist).

2. Establish clear rules and boundaries that are designed to safeguard student rights. These should include, but not be limited to, each person taking a turn, speaking respectfully, speaking only for himself or herself, not interrupting others, and so on.

3. Do not force children to disclose personal information beyond what they are comfortable with. Casualties are most likely to occur when people do more than they are ready to do.

4. Because peer pressure is so strong among children, the individual rights of each participant need to be protected.

5. Remain sensitive to cultural differences in the ways children from various backgrounds respond in groups like this.

6. Understand clearly that there are specific times when you as a leader must intervene in order to protect the safety of the children and to ensure that your groups run smoothly.

WHEN TO INTERVENE IN GROUPS

Research on effective group leadership has identified instances when you will need to do something specific to prevent people from getting hurt or to move the process along. We recommend that you memorize this list, or at least keep it close enough to refer to, until you log considerable experience as a process-oriented group leader. Intervention is called for under the following circumstances:

1. *To stop abusive behavior or hostility.* It is never permissible for group members to be disrespectful or abusive toward one another. Whenever you witness that one or more children are treating others in ways that may be hurtful, you must step in to help redirect the tone: "Candy, how might you tell Frank the same thing, but this time in a way that will not hurt his feelings? Then, perhaps you, Frank, could tell Candy how you are feeling right now."

2. *To enforce rules upon which everyone has agreed.* The usual way of beginning any process group is to create and negotiate rules of conduct regarding behavior that is acceptable and behavior that is not. Generally, some guidelines are developed regarding confidentiality, speaking only for oneself, and being respectful and caring during interactions, to name a few. The leader's role is not so much to enforce these rules as to ensure that group members comply with them: "I notice that Danny has come in late again. How does everyone want to handle this?"

3. *To cut off distractions and digressions.* Because group time is so valuable and there is so much to do, the leader serves an important function by keeping things on track and not permitting any single member to dominate or control discussions. Some students also need direct feedback regarding their interpersonal styles that may be irritating or counterproductive: "Dana, I notice that you were rolling your eyes skyward as Jon was talking. Perhaps you could be helpful to him and let him know how you react when he takes so long to get his points across."

4. *To model appropriate ways of being.* One of the most powerful roles you can play as a teacher in general, and a group leader in particular, is to demonstrate the ways in which you want children to act. This modeling can take place in the ways you present yourself, the skills you demonstrate, the confidence and serenity you exude, or even the language you use to express yourself: "Notice that I just said that I upset myself over what just happened, meaning that nobody else did this to me; I did it to myself based on the way I interpreted the situation. When I speak like that, I am reminding myself that, ultimately, I am in control of how I choose to feel."

5. *To spice up boredom or passivity.* Groups can become predictable and stale without some intervention on the part of the leader to stir things up occasionally. In fact, there is probably no condition that has turned off more students to education than tedious sessions. There are no limits to the creative actions you can take to breathe some life into a group—using humor, spontaneous actions, role-playing, almost anything to get

children's energy flowing: "Okay, you guys are acting like you are asleep. Let's try something a little different. I want each one of you to pretend to be someone else in this group for the next 15 minutes, but don't say who you are imitating. Let's see if any of us can recognize ourselves."

6. *To correct irrational or distorted thinking.* In one of the previous examples, we mentioned that the language people use is symptomatic of what they are thinking inside. By changing the ways we talk to ourselves, we also change our perceptions and subsequent actions based on these interpretations. It is thus common for group leaders to intervene when children speak in self-defeating or irrational ways:

Externalizing: *"How can I do better in school when everyone else is try-ing to sabotage me?"*

Exaggerating: *"This is the worst day of my life; it is the worst day that I will ever have in my life."*

Self-judging: *"I am the worst soccer player who ever lived. I'm so bad I'll never be good at anything."*

Denying responsibility: *"It's not my fault. I just have bad luck."*

Distorting: *"If I don't get what I want, I'll just die."*

In each case, the group leader jumps in to correct the way the student is expressing him- or herself: "You mean that if you don't get what you want, you will be slightly disappointed."

7. *To reinforce disclosures.* Similar to classroom behavior modification, whenever a child does something that we want to continue, and want other children to imitate, we reinforce that behavior. "Tammy, I really like the way you just asserted yourself, and yet you did so in a very diplomatic and gentle way." We may also wish to systematically support behaviors such as disclosing, being direct and concise, cooperating, caring, and tak-ing constructive risks.

8. *To provide structure as needed.* Groups flounder when they have either too much structure or not enough direction. Initially, when teachers make the transition from the classroom to process group settings, they tend to be too controlling in trying to ensure a successful experience. There are also times when groups meander because participants are not sure what is expected. Generally, it is better to provide more structure in the beginning stages of groups and then eventually allow children to assume more and more responsibility for where things go.

9. *To stop complaining.* Once children feel safe, it does not take long for things to turn into a gripe session. Kids will complain about other teachers,

their parents, the weather, lost opportunities, or any number of other possibilities, and this litany of injustices is often not helpful. One rule we like
is to talk only about things about which we can do something: "David, I
appreciate the fact that it is hard for you with the reputation that you have
created. We can't do anything about the past now, nor can we stop other
people from saying what they like about you, but we sure can help you to
act differently in the future. Let's concentrate on that instead."

10. *To comfort someone who is feeling anxious.* At times, we sense the
beginning signs that a child is really struggling with something. Tears are
on the verge of flowing. We observe agitation or withdrawal or anger
seething. Intervention is sometimes required to make sure that a child feels
supported: "Donny, you look like you are having a really hard time right
now. How can we help you?"

11. *To confront inconsistencies.* Direct confrontation is in order when
someone is doing something that is self-defeating or self-contradicting.
Although we might model these interventions initially, after a while
children pick up the tune, and then they can do the work themselves, especially with cues from the leader: "Cassandra, you look puzzled by what
Nathan is saying, as if something doesn't fit right with what he said earlier. Why don't you tell him what you heard?"

12. *To give constructive feedback.* Similar to modeling direct confrontation when indicated, we also want to demonstrate ways to give others the
benefit of how we observe them. After we have given such feedback a few
times, children pick up the behavior and continue doing it for one another.
Ideally, feedback is most constructive when it meets the following criteria:

> *Specific.* There is nothing more useless then giving feedback that is
> so general that it is meaningless. This type of "yearbook feedback"
> is similar to what kids write in each other's yearbooks: "You're so
> sweet. Don't ever change." That may feel good for a few minutes,
> but after the effect wears off, you have nothing left with which to
> work. Therefore, rather than saying to someone, "You aren't taken
> seriously," you might say more specifically, "I notice that when you
> speak, you use a soft tone of voice and rarely look at anyone, and
> others seem to discount what you're saying."

> *Sensitive.* Feedback is often threatening—very threatening. It is
> indeed scary to hear people tell you honestly what they think about
> you. For that reason, you want to be very careful about the way
> comments are phrased so the student can really hear what is said
> and take it in. "One of the things you do that I really appreciate,
> Mina, is the understated way you express yourself. There is such
> power behind your words. I wonder, though, if you might project
> more of yourself when you speak." Good feedback is thus coupled

with something supportive and something constructive (notice that we've avoided the use of words like *positive* and *negative*).

Supportive. Not only should you provide emotional support for those receiving feedback, but you should also strengthen comments with supporting examples. Whenever possible, it is useful to provide an illustration of the behavior you are identifying. "Just now, Dominick, you made a sour expression with your face when others were saying things with which you obviously disagreed. See? You're doing it right now. What happens to me when I see that is that I start to feel that you aren't listening and then I stop trying."

Although all of these examples are those of teachers providing the feedback, in actuality, they are facilitating the students giving one another helpful suggestions. The teacher, cast in the role of an authority figure, often has so much power and control that feedback is often far more accessible from peers. That is not to say, however, that you don't model the kind of communications that you want others to give.

Each of these group process interventions is added to the repertoire of skills we have already reviewed in previous chapters. It is just as appropriate for you to reflect feelings and content or summarize what people say at various junctures in groups as in individual sessions.

VARIETIES OF GROUP PROCESS

Teachers routinely incorporate group process activities into their curricula in a number of ways. They do so to spice up their classes; supplement academic learning with emotional growth experiences; and help children deal with the important issues with which they are struggling, such as peer acceptance, personal identity, values clarification, moral and emotional development, relationship problems, stress management, and other adjustment difficulties that are part of daily life.

Teachers employ process structures because they recognize that a number of students are struggling with similar issues. One child approaches you because she is upset about a friend whose mother was killed in a car accident, but you have noticed that several others seem to have been profoundly affected. Some children seem more reticent than usual. Others have been acting out more than normal. Several parents have also reported that their children have expressed an unusual amount of worry about their safety. In such circumstances, teachers sense that talking about the accident openly, especially in relation to children's fears, would be appropriate. This is just one example of how a process group experience might be used to help children clarify and express their feelings. Other examples of process groups follow.

Structured Group Activities

These kinds of exercises are quite familiar to teachers who want to help students personalize class material. They can be as simple as dividing a class into subgroups to discuss how they feel about a film they viewed, a book they read, or music they heard; or they can be as elaborate as a series of structured simulation exercises that takes place throughout a week, semester, or year. Usually, specific outcomes are desired, ones that help children achieve greater self-awareness and understanding of others.

Imagine, for example, that a social studies teacher is presenting a unit on discrimination. She might give her students a series of activities designed to help them become aware of their own prejudices and how such attitudes develop. An art teacher might show her students a painting and ask them to respond to it aesthetically.

The *tribes* model of cooperative learning is based on a set of structured group norms that emphasizes sharing personal concerns and feelings, expressing positive regard for one another, and working as a team to complete assigned tasks. Rules are established for all interactions in which (a) confidentiality is enforced, (b) attentive listening to one another is required, (c) negative remarks are avoided, and (d) participants have the right to personal privacy. These group norms are intended to create a "tribal" community among students that makes it safe to explore new areas; express creativity; and develop intimacy without fear of criticism, rejection, or failure.

Consistent with process groups, responsibility is shifted from the teacher to the students to enforce the rules, draw one another out in discussion, and initiate interaction. The teacher's role is to facilitate the process by providing structure, exploring issues, asking questions, introducing activities, and assigning tasks as indicated. The goals are to encourage responsible and caring behavior.

Fishbowl Structures

The teacher works with a smaller group of children in the middle of the room with the rest of the class forming a circle around them. The observers may be assigned a partner inside the group to observe and give feedback to afterward, or they may be given certain observational tasks regarding the group process itself.

The participants inside the fishbowl are afforded a more intimate experience in which they demonstrate principles that the observers can also learn vicariously. After a round of this, observers and participants switch roles.

A class of high school students was invited to explore gender differences in a dramatic way. The girls in the class were invited into the fishbowl and instructed to pretend that they were boys sitting around doing and talking about whatever they think boys do when they get together.

Before too long, they were playing out exaggerated roles of boys talking about football and sex, acting like macho jocks, and laughing uproariously throughout the discussion.

When the boys' turn came to act like a group of girls getting together, they, too, played their roles to the hilt, strutting and preening the way they imagined that feminine, helpless girls would act. Needless to say, the girls observing the scenario outside the fishbowl were no more amused than the boys were when they watched the girls mocking them.

A spirited discussion then ensued with the class at large, with both boys and girls talking about how they felt trapped by their sex roles. They expressed their resentment at being ridiculed and resolved to be more sensitive to gender differences in the future.

Guidance Groups

If school counselors had the time, the resources, and the support staff, they would devote most of their time to guidance groups and hence reap the most benefits for children. Kids need help with many areas that are not part of the academic curriculum. In fact, if you asked children to make a list of the subjects that they would most like to study if they could create their own curriculum, we probably would not see English, mathematics, social studies, science, history, foreign language, and humanities at the tops of their lists, at least as they are conventionally taught. Instead, we might hear that they would prefer to learn about the opposite sex, relationships (what makes them work and what makes them fall apart), parents (how to get them to do your bidding), and other topics of timely interest.

Guidance groups are geared toward supplementing children's learning in academic subjects with specialized training in more pragmatic areas of immediate interest. This format is more familiar to you than many of the other kinds of groups because it offers primarily didactic instruction. Whether designed to address problem-solving or study skills, career exploration, or communication skills, this group format allows you to present practical information about a subject of great interest to children and then help them individualize what they learned to their own unique situations.

Support Groups

A group of teachers in one school district became alarmed by the number of children who reported violence in their neighborhoods. The teachers observed that many of the academic and discipline problems they encountered seemed to be triggered by what the children were experiencing in their communities. With the counselors in their district overworked and understaffed, the teachers resolved to institute several measures to address the problem.

Support groups were organized in the schools under the guidance of a few counselors who recognized that teachers often had a much better handle on the daily lives of children. The teachers were prepared and trained as teams of two coleaders and assigned to begin support groups in their schools. In addition to the problem of violence, another major problem was identified in the area of drug/alcohol abuse (by children or their parents). Groups were thus targeted to these two different interest areas and followed a curriculum that consisted of providing opportunities for students to talk about their common concerns; receive feedback from one another about what works and what doesn't; learn that they are not alone in their struggles and that others share their fears and apprehensions; and, finally, lend support to each other during these times of stress.

GETTING SUPPORT FOR YOURSELF

The best way to learn to lead process groups is to recruit a partner who knows more than you do. With a more experienced coleader, you will appease many of your justifiable apprehensions about venturing into this unknown territory and also provide yourself a safety net for when the going gets tough. A coleader can model alternative ways to begin, maintain, and end group experiences. He or she can also give you valuable feedback after each session regarding aspects of your leadership style that you can work to improve.

Whether you find this partner among your own staff—a counselor, administrator, or another teacher—or you invite someone from the local university to supervise you in the field, a coleader will give you the added boost of confidence and support necessary when undertaking an exciting yet frightening new adventure.

RESPONDING TO CRITICAL INCIDENTS IN THE CLASSROOM

One final application of the skills you've learned is centered on typical interactions in your classroom. Experienced teachers have learned over time that when students ask questions, make statements, or engage in certain behaviors, it is best to interpret what is really being communicated before they respond. In this manner, just like during individual sessions, you are able to deal not only with the content of what is being said but also the underlying feelings.

Based on our experience as teachers in a variety of settings, we have collected the following favorite interventions for responding to students in class. Although technically not group techniques because they respond to individual students, these interventions are intended as much for the audience as for the person speaking. Although some of these might appear to be clever gimmicks to be memorized, in each case they demonstrate certain values that you may wish to model for your students— openness, honesty, directness, caring, and consistency.

Following is a list of responses to particular incidents, questions, statements, or actions that occur in most classrooms:

- *"Good question. What do you think?"*
  When a student asks you a question to which you don't know the answer.

- *"What evidence do you have to support that belief?"*
  When a student is misguided or wrong.

- *"Don't tell me. Show me."*
  When you don't understand what is being said. When the class needs energy.

- *"Don't argue with me. Argue with yourself."*
  When a student challenges you. When you feel resistance to a new idea you are presenting.

- *"I'll get back to you on that."*
  When you don't know how to respond to a question.

- *"Take a wild guess."*
  When a student says, "I don't know."

- *"That's a good point. Now, how would you relate it to our discussion?"*
  When a student is wandering or distracting.

- *"I wonder if you would mind summarizing your main point."*
  When the student is rambling. When your attention wandered and you didn't hear what was said.

- *"You're looking awfully reflective."*
  When a student is quiet or passive.

- *"Count off by threes."*
  When there is low energy in the class, you divide them into small groups to discuss something provocative.

- *"That reminds me of a story."*
  When students appear puzzled by what you are saying and need to connect it to their experience.

- *"I wonder how you could say that differently."*
  When students are being insensitive or disrespectful.

- *"Can I talk to you during the break?"*
  When a student monopolizes or demands attention.

- *"Do you really agree with what I just said?"*
  When students are approval seeking.

- *"How do you think you did?"*
  When a student asks how he or she did on a paper, report, assignment, or activity.

- *"Well, not exactly."*
  When a student's skill levels are miserable.

- *"What's it like for you to be here right now?"*
  When things aren't clicking.

- *"What do you need right now?"*
  When a student is obviously having a hard time or breaks down in some way.

- *"Let's try something else."*
  When whatever you're doing isn't working.

- *"I'm aware that something is going on between us that I'd like to work out."*
  When someone is being consistently annoying or disruptive.

- *"I wonder what this is really about?"* (spoken to yourself)
  When a student pushes your buttons.

- *"I've got a problem."*
  When a student tests boundaries (comes late, leaves early, skips class, turns in assignments late, and so on).

This, of course, is a mere sampling of things that come up in any class. These responses are hardly carved in stone. They are merely intended to demonstrate the ways that you can face challenges directly without losing your cool. They also show ways that you can introduce process elements into even the most content-driven lesson. For example, even conducting a unit on fractions or indirect pronouns still brings up emotional issues in children. Stopping to ask occasionally how they're feeling inside will often bring up a number of issues related to feeling dumb or proud. Students can address how they handle frustration from being bored or not understanding the new material or being embarrassed when they make a mistake. This will help create a safe emotional environment, one in which students will feel more comfortable asking one another for help. It takes only a few minutes to address some of these concerns and make it safer in class to admit when you don't know what's going on.

SUGGESTED ACTIVITIES

1. Observe the dynamics and processes that take place in the groups to which you currently belong: at school, work, home, and play. What characteristic roles do you play in these groups? What are your strengths and weaknesses as a group member and potential leader? Note these reactions in a journal or share them aloud in a group discussion.

2. Select a structured group activity that accesses children's values, feelings, and beliefs, especially an activity that you would feel comfortable implementing. Try out this activity with a group of children, classmates, or friends. Solicit feedback from them afterward as to what they liked and disliked about the experience.

3. Identify someone who has experience leading groups and who may agree to work with you as a coleader of a support group. Approach the person (e.g., a school counselor, school psychologist, school social worker, senior colleague with advanced training, counselor educator from the local university) with a plan for the kind of group you might like to run.

4. Meet in a group with your peers and share experiences you have had as members of process groups. What did you learn from these experiences? What specific things did the leader(s) do that you most and least appreciated?

SUGGESTED READING

Beaudoin, M. N., & Taylor, M. (2004). *Breaking the culture of bullying and disrespect, grades K–8.* Thousand Oaks, CA: Corwin Press.

Boynton, M., & Boynton, C. (2005). *The educator's guide to preventing and solving discipline problems.* Alexandria, VA: Association for Supervision and Curriculum Development.

Corey, G., & Corey, M. S. (2005). *Groups: Process and practice* (7th ed.). Belmont, CA: Wadsworth.

Franek, M. (2005). Foiling cyberbullies in the new wild wild west. *Educational Leadership, 63*(4), 39–43.

Gibbs, J. (1987). *Tribes: A process of social development and cooperative learning.* Santa Rosa, CA: Center Source.

Iverson, A. M. (2003). *Building competence in classroom management and discipline* (4th ed.). Upper Saddle River, NJ: Pearson Education.

Kottler, E., & Gallavan, N. P. (2007). *Secrets to success for beginning elementary school teachers.* Thousand Oaks, CA: Corwin Press.

Kreidler, W. M. (2005). *Creative conflict resolution.* Parsippany, NJ: Good Year Books.

Marzano, R. J., Marzano, J. S., & Pickering, D. J. (2003). *Classroom management that works: Research-based strategies for every teacher.* Alexandria, VA: American Counseling Association.

O'Moore, M. (2004). *Dealing with bullying in schools.* London: Paul Chapman.

Ray, R. G. (1999). *The facilitative leader.* Upper Saddle River, NJ: Prentice Hall.

Roberts, W. B. (2006). *Bullying from both sides: Strategic interventions for working with bullies and victims.* Thousand Oaks, CA: Corwin Press.

Stone, R. (2005). *Best classroom management practices for reaching all learners: What award-winning classroom teachers do.* Thousand Oaks, CA: Corwin Press.

Communicating With Parents

6

One of the most frustrating aspects of a teaching job is recognizing, in spite of all your best efforts and devotion to children's learning and welfare, there is actually little you can do without the cooperation of parents. Children are in your charge long enough for you to influence them in significant ways. Unfortunately, once they leave school, they may be in a distinctly different environment and culture that works at counter-purposes to what has been accomplished in school.

Jonas is among your most talented students—the best and the brightest. There is no doubt that college is in his future, and after that, who knows? He is smart enough and personable enough to do anything he sets his mind to do.

Away from school, however, there are quite different forces at work. Jonas lives in a house with his mother, a half-dozen other children who are related to him in some way, and his mother's current lover. He is teased mercilessly by his half-siblings when he brings a book home. If he wants to read or study, there is no way he can do it with the chaos in his house—television blaring, kids fighting, mother and lover arguing, people coming and going. Jonas spends as little time at home as possible.

Jonas's mother knows her son is bright and has potential. She is doing the best she can to raise her children, mostly by herself. How dare those teachers insinuate that she doesn't care about her son, or any of her children for that matter? What is this notice about another one of those teacher conferences? She'll show those know-it-all teachers this time. No way will she sit and listen to another lecture on "reading at home" or "sending her son to a special summer camp program." Maybe she'll just move to some other place where people will get off her back. It would be the best thing for Jonas anyway.

WHEN THE CHILD SAVES THE PARENTS

Without parental cooperation, teachers can do little to help enrich children's lives. One of the most important tasks a teacher can accomplish is to recruit parents as partners in the educational process. Yes, developing trusting relationships with children is the main part of our job, but unless we can do the same with their parents, our educational and helping efforts will be limited.

One of the more interesting areas of psychological research in the past few decades has been family systems—that is, recognizing the powerful forces at work in the relationships between parents and children. We now know that it is senseless to try to understand the actions of an individual child without examining the family context in which they take place. There are coalitions in families, hidden sources of power, and subtle lines of communication that motivate and inadvertently reinforce behavior behind the scenes.

Previously, Larry had been a very cooperative young man in school, but recently, he developed a number of irritating mannerisms that invariably got under his teacher's skin. He was sent to the counselor for help and then later referred to a therapist in the community because of the apparent severity of his problems. The therapist saw Larry for only a few sessions before there was remarkable improvement and Larry became his old self once again.

A few weeks later, the therapist was again contacted by the school system, but this time it was about Larry's younger brother, Stephen, who had been caught setting off the school's fire alarm. This was especially puzzling because prior to this incident, Stephen had been a model student—straight A's and a leader in his class. Again, in a remarkably brief period of time, Stephen responded to counseling and resolved to stay out of trouble in the future. A few weeks later, the therapist was again contacted, but this time by the parents directly; they were having trouble with their youngest son, who was acting surly and belligerent around the house. "What has gotten into our children?" the parents asked. "They never had these problems before."

What indeed? Eventually, it was learned that the parents were having marital problems that had escalated to the point that open warfare was taking place in the house. Screams of outrage and slammed doors punctuated the household on a regular basis as the two parents continuously badgered one another and threatened to walk out. About the only time they seemed to get along was when one of their children was in trouble. In such instances, they would temporarily call a truce and pool their efforts out of concern for their children. In one dramatic example of this phenomenon, the parents were arguing at the dinner table over which one was really at fault for their collective misery. Just before the argument escalated into a major conflict, Larry tossed a roll across the table at one of his younger brothers. Soon, all four of them were involved in the skirmish, requiring the parents to stop arguing in order to put down the disturbance.

This pattern of a child acting out in order to distract the parents from their own troubles is not unusual. Although not usually a conscious action, the effects are nevertheless quite powerful: As long as the child is having problems in school, the parents join forces in order to be of assistance; once the child straightens out, the parental conflicts or other family skirmishes resume. The child's acting-out behavior thus serves as a stabilizing function within the family.

The implications of these family dynamics are profound for teachers who wish to understand why certain children are troubled and why they are inexplicably acting out with no apparent gain. This example can also help you understand the crucial nature of parent-teacher communication: Unless you can coordinate what you are doing with the people with whom the children live, your best efforts may fall short. Thus, as dreaded as it may be for some teachers, communicating with parents represents your best opportunity to gather important information about your children's family situations and, sometimes, to even have constructive influence on parents' behavior so that they may support more effectively what you are doing, and vice versa.

There are three primary instances in which teachers communicate with parents on a regular basis: during an open house arranged by the school, at scheduled conferences, and during phone calls home. In each case, the same counseling skills introduced earlier will be invaluable to keep these conversations productive and focused. You will use the same strategies with parents as you do with children: establish a solid relationship, get them to talk about their views on matters, reflect their underlying feelings, show them you hear and understand their concerns, set limits as needed, establish mutual goals, and construct a collaborative plan for making desired changes.

OPEN HOUSE

Let's take the easiest forum first because it provides the most structure. Many school districts schedule an open house for parents to visit sometime early in the school year. The intent is to give parents an overview of their children's schedule and activities, as well as to provide opportunities to meet teachers. This is a great idea, in theory; unfortunately, chaos often results, with parents and kids running all over the place while teachers try to keep some sort of order.

In most cases, you will have only a few minutes to spend with each group of parents, or sometimes a few parents at a time. Therefore, it is very important to make a good first impression. You want to appear confident, poised, and knowledgeable, but without seeming arrogant and unapproachable. Basically, what you are trying to do in the limited time is make yourself as attractive as you possibly can so that parents will be open to talking with you in the future, when such interactions will be useful.

Probably the most important thing you can do in your presentations to parents is to come across as enthusiastic about your teaching and caring toward their children. Although it will appear as if your main goal is to cover content related to your expectations and rules for class, as well as what you will be doing throughout the year, keep in mind that parents are checking you out carefully to see if you are the type of person they are willing to trust. There will be many times when the kids will come home complaining about you to their parents (your work is too hard, you're boring, you're not fair, you hate them, you dress like a dork, and so on). If you have managed to recruit parents as allies, they will stop such whining and support your efforts.

PHONING HOME

The most common, accessible, and easiest means of consulting with parents is through phone calls home. This has the advantage of being informal, less threatening, and more convenient than having to schedule appointments. On the other hand, such calls are usually made during the evenings, which cuts into your private time.

Many teachers begin the school year with an initial call home. They introduce themselves to parents and tell a little bit about their expectations and plans for the forthcoming year. Although this may be time-consuming, it allows you to cover things that won't have to be dealt with during the open house.

In general, keep in mind that telephone conferences are most successful when providing positive feedback and identifying minor problems. This method is useful for keeping parents up to date on events of the school day and for giving short progress reports or follow-up information.

Examples of this type of phone communication follow:

- "I wanted to let you know that I missed Maya in class earlier in the week. She is so helpful to me in class."
- "I wanted to alert you that your son will have daily homework assignments for the next few weeks. So far, he's doing well, and I want to make sure that we can keep the progress going."
- "I just wanted you to know that your daughter played a major role in our discussion today. I know she's usually quiet, but she said some really important things. I was quite impressed."
- "Your son has so much energy and enthusiasm. I notice that he gets a little carried away at times, though, especially after lunch, when he eats a lot of candy. I was wondering if you've noticed anything similar at home?"

All of the counseling skills presented previously come into play during these calls to a student's home. Because you can't rely on nonverbal attending behaviors to communicate your interest, it is even more important to use verbal acknowledgments to let the parents know that you are following them. This might sound rather elementary to mention, but you'd be surprised how important little things can be to producing a positive experience. Remember, you have just a few minutes to make a good impression, communicate your message, and gather whatever information you are searching for. Also, keep in mind that you don't know how good your timing is at the moment you called; make sure that the parents are receptive and available before you launch into your conversation. If not, ask for a convenient time to call back.

Basically, there are several reasons why you would call home:

1. To let the parents know their child did something you very much appreciate: *"Your son was such a help to me today. When other kids started acting up, he got them to quiet down. I just wanted you to know what an influential leader he can be."*

2. To inform parents of an academic achievement: *"Your daughter received a grade of 95 percent on the unit test she took yesterday in class. That's the best she's done so far!"*

3. To gather information you need in order to do your job: *"Your daughter tells me that she has problems concentrating and that she has seen specialists about this. Could you fill me in on what's going on and what advice you have for helping her?"*

4. To recruit parent support when a student is noncompliant: *"Although your child has great potential, it doesn't look like he's going to pass unless he starts turning in assignments."*

5. To alert the parent regarding a change in behavior you've observed: *"I've noticed the twins seemed a little tired this week. I was wondering if they were sick, or if something has happened recently that they are concerned about."*

Because of parent work schedules and family times in the evening, many teachers prefer to call in the morning after the child has left home and before school starts in order to catch the parent before he or she leaves for work.

Before you call a parent, find a quiet space in which you have some telephone privacy. Confidentiality should not be compromised. Make sure you have plenty of time for a conversation. If you feel you might be rushed, postpone the call until later. Prepare your opening statement. Make a list of the main points you want to cover. You will want to describe what has transpired in the past and the nature of the resulting successes or failures, and identify goals for the future. Have specific examples identified to describe. It will be helpful to have your grade/attendance book and examples of work handy for reference if necessary.

When phoning home, it is important to begin the conversation by introducing yourself and setting a positive tone for the conversation. Be pleasant and polite. Speak in objective terms when describing the current situation. Give the reason for the call. Ask the parent to provide any information that might be useful or pertinent to the situation. Remember, you are seeking the parent's support and help.

In complicated situations, you may receive an emotional and/or defensive reaction. At this point, counseling skills will be useful to reflect the anger you hear and summarize the points being made. You will need to give the parent time to express his or her point of view. Remember to restate what you hear and reflect underlying feelings. Try to guide the conversation to how to make a difference in the future. Enlist the aid of the parent to continue to support what has been working for the student or to help the student make changes in the future.

Parents need plenty of opportunity to ask questions, request clarification, and look for alternative solutions to problems. They are vested partners in the process of helping the student achieve personal, social, and academic success at school. Brainstorm with parents as to possible future scenarios. Coordinate your efforts with parents to create a workable plan.

To bring the telephone call to a close, first summarize the main points of the conversation, and then check for understanding with the parent/guardian. Finally, determine a time in the future to call back for follow-up and evaluation.

If the conversation becomes confrontational, uncomfortable, and/or unproductive, it may be best to end the telephone communication. You can explain diplomatically that your time is limited and make plans for a face-to-face conference (with or without an administrator or counselor present). Make sure after the call is over that you write out a short summary of what transpired, what was agreed, and when you will call back for follow-up.

ELECTRONIC COMMUNICATION

One alternative, or supplement, to phone conversations is to communicate with parents via e-mail. Electronic messages are great for instant feedback on a job well done and short progress reports. Watch your spelling and punctuation. Remember, too, that you can't always be sure that this form of communication will be received and read immediately. Confidentiality can also be a problem, so it's best to check with parents before sending an electronic message. It is also wise to keep in mind that you are providing a written record of your remarks that could someday be used for purposes you never imagined.

Web pages and blog sites can also be extremely useful as a way to communicate with parents, as well as to keep them informed about projects going on in your classroom. Group or individual projects, and newsletters, can be displayed on the Web so that parents and friends might access the information.

PARENT-TEACHER CONFERENCES

Sitting on the top of the memos and announcements in the Spanish teacher's school mailbox was a parent conference request form from Susie's mother. Susie, a ninth-grade student, was a quiet girl who kept pretty much to herself. Although she was a cheerleader, she did not really mingle with the other students. She was dependable, always had her books and a pencil in class, and received average grades. With a soft voice, Susie responded when called on, participated in activities, and never talked out of turn. Any teacher would have been happy to have her in class. Her Spanish teacher could only wonder at the purpose of this conference.

She began to get organized for the meeting during her preparation period. First, she pulled out a copy of her course description, which included class expectations and grading procedures. Then, she made a list of all the assignments, quizzes, and tests she had given, along with Susie's grades. Next, she gathered examples of Susie's work to show her mother, followed by a collection of the forthcoming assignments. Finally, the teacher looked at the list of parents who had signed in at the open house to see if Susie's mother had attended and checked her telephone file cards to see if she had ever talked to her before for any reason. She had learned long ago that preparation was extremely important before meeting with any parent.

After school, the teacher rearranged the furniture in the room, placing two student desks together so they would face one another. She organized all the materials and then sat anxiously wondering what was on Mrs. Tanner's mind. She found out soon enough. During the course of the conference, she learned that it had been Susie's decision to take Spanish despite her mother and counselor's preference that she wait until 10th grade. In addition, Mrs. Tanner revealed that her daughter was a competitive swimmer with a state ranking who would miss many days of school while participating in meets. She was concerned about Susie's grades. The teacher continued to listen and encouraged the parent to talk: She learned that Susie was indeed very shy in certain situations, even though she was a cheerleader. Mrs. Tanner's conference provided the teacher with additional insight and background information into her student's behavior. She developed an appreciation of Susie's goals and determination to reach those goals. She was in a better position to help Susie in the future. This involved meeting with her individually to review and practice material presented in class, schedule makeup assignments, and make sure she was comfortable in class before including her in discussions.

Frequently, the thought of a parent-teacher conference puts the teacher on the defensive. Questions like, "What does this parent want from me?" and "Who does this parent think he is?" come to mind. We prepare a list of retorts, such as, "I do not give too many homework assignments," "My tests are not too hard," and "I do not pick on your son." Yet more often than not, conferences are helpful and motivating. Parents want their children to do well. They want teachers to help their children. The information that they give provides you with important insights that allow you to plan accordingly. The teacher in the previous example learned of topics that she could use to draw Susie into class participation. Furthermore, a team effort can help ensure that a student stays on the path to success.

Mrs. Robert came to see her son's fourth-grade teacher after an unsatisfactory progress report had been sent home. Rudy was failing, and his behavior in school was erratic. Mrs. Robert told the teacher at the beginning of the conference that if her son misbehaved, to go ahead and beat him because that's what she did at home. The teacher suggested that perhaps they might talk about other alternatives, because physical punishment is often not very effective, and even when it does work, there are certain negative side effects. But first, she reviewed with Mrs. Robert what the expectations were for school and which materials Rudy was to bring each day.

Once a collaborative relationship was established, Mrs. Robert was more than willing to explore ways that she might help. In the course of the conversation, Mrs. Robert told the teacher that Rudy was the youngest in the family. (Did being "babied" contribute to his immature behavior? the teacher wondered.) Her two older sons were attending college. Rudy's ambition was to be a singer. Even in fourth grade, he had been selected for the boy's choir, a rare honor. Now, there was a talent that the teacher could put to use. She made a note to involve singing in her lesson plans the next day. Maybe she could challenge Rudy to learn through music and channel some of his energy.

In both examples, the benefits of parent-teacher conferences are highlighted:

1. To gather helpful information about the child's interests and abilities

2. To observe the family dynamics in action and note clues that might explain a child's behavior

3. To recruit the parents' assistance as partners in the educational process

4. To work in concert with parents to achieve mutually agreed-upon goals

DIRECTING A CONSTRUCTIVE CONFERENCE

In many ways, a parent-teacher conference is like an improvisational play: There is a general script to follow but with lots of room for spontaneous action. You are the director as well as one of the main characters. The parents and child form the rest of the cast, although they may be unclear about their roles. Each of you is probably rehearsing a part in anticipation of what the other might say or do. Careful thought will need to be given to every facet of the production in order for the performance to go smoothly.

Setting the Stage

Just as there are different kinds of plays—dramas, musicals, comedies—so is there an assortment of parent-teacher conferences, each with its own unique plot development and script structure. Essentially, conferences come about in three ways: (a) those initiated by the parent (if there is a perceived problem), (b) those initiated by the teacher (if a consultation might help to gather information or solicit assistance), and (c) those initiated by the system (regularly scheduled meetings each semester). Depending on who initiates the meeting, the goals will be somewhat different. In the case of conferences requested by parents, you will rely primarily on listening skills by inviting parents to discuss their concerns. Those scheduled by you will involve more questioning and information gathering on your part, as well as goal setting or problem solving. The kind that involve routine reports on progress will be the most structured of all, and in these, you will work on establishing a good alliance with the parents, leading a focused discussion, and dispensing information on the student's social and academic progress.

In all circumstances, it is important to use language with which the parents will be comfortable. If you use educational terms, be sure to define them and use examples. Avoid labeling. Speak of the child as an individual without stereotyping. Use accurate descriptions. Don't gloss over problems to avoid conflict.

In setting the stage for each of these conferences, you will consider a number of questions: When and where will the conference be held? How long will the conference be? Try not to schedule appointments too close together if it can be avoided.

Who will be participating? Will an interpreter be needed? Will other team teachers be included? Will the student be present?

Some teachers like to include the student in the process. Rather than being "on trial," the student can be an active participant in the planning process, often giving valuable input and insight. In discussion prior to the conference, these are a few questions you may consider asking the student: "What are some things you would like to accomplish in this meeting with your parents?" or "What role would you like me to play as a mediator?" or even "How will you react when I mention those disturbances that occurred in class?" The student is not only warned about what will occur but can come to view the meeting with shared responsibility for its successful outcome.

Some teachers are instituting student-led conferences, wherein the student takes responsibility for all stages—from planning to chairing the conference—and develops leadership skills along the way. The student enjoys the attention received from parent(s) and teacher in this positive, constructive environment. The teacher works with the student in developing the communication skills needed and collecting a portfolio of student work to present at the conference. The teacher finds the amount of work she has to do in preparation for the conference is lessened, and her role in the conference shifts from leader to resource person.

At times, it is inappropriate to include the student, such as when there is a serious problem in the home, when control issues are dominant, or when there is a serious problem in the classroom. Remember that each additional person adds another dimension to the relationships operating at the conference.

In staging the setting for the conference, regardless of who leads it, consider where the furniture is placed—sitting behind a desk can create a symbolic barrier. A face-to-face position will lend itself to a more cooperative and sharing atmosphere. You will need comfortable seats for all the people attending the conference. The location of the meeting also needs to be considered; try to find a place with the least amount of distractions. (You can always post a note on the door asking not to be disturbed.) If you need to be conscious of the time, place a clock in an inconspicuous place.

As far as props go, you will want a portfolio of the student's work, grades, and assignments. If feasible, include videotapes or photographs of the student involved in activities in your room. You should make an effort to include samples of the child's best work so that you can begin the meeting on a positive note. You might also prepare a list of questions that you have about the student and a loose script of what you hope to accomplish.

The Introduction

If this is the first conference with the individual, greet the parent at the office and introduce yourself to him or her. Shake hands and make eye contact. Comment on how glad you are the parent was able to come to the conference as a way of making your guest welcome. As you guide the parent to the meeting room, begin the conversation with a positive comment about the student. "He always says hello to me in the morning." "She does her homework very neatly." "Billy told me he just got his Water Safety Instruction card. You must be very proud of him."

Give the parent a moment to look around the room and get his or her bearings. You might give a tour as you describe the activities of a typical day. This may be the parent's first time seeing what his or her child has alluded to at home.

Some schools have group conferences where all the student's teachers and a counselor or administrator are present. In this situation, common modes of behavior and objectives can be identified, and consistent feedback and monitoring can be established. A level of expected improvement can be set with all present for consistency.

Teachers can work together to establish common goals with incremental steps that all teachers can watch for so that the student won't be overwhelmed, yet at the same time, a change in behavior for the positive is emphasized—whether it be comportment or academic achievement. This can result in a cohesive plan.

Interaction Begins

A good way to move the meeting along is to direct the conversation to the purpose of the conference. If this is basically an informational session, you can give your report on the child's progress. If problems have been identified, you might start by asking a general, open-ended question about (or to) the child: "What has Judy said about school at home?" Use your listening and exploration skills to seek information about the student that only a parent could provide. If the student is present, give him or her an opportunity to talk, ask questions, and state his or her feelings.

Problem Solving

Describe the student's behavior and schoolwork, pointing out his or her strengths and weaknesses. Identify objectives or goals for the semester. Stay away from educational jargon. Ask the student to describe his or her own perception of the problem. What obstacles does the student see? What solutions can he or she suggest that will change and hopefully improve the situation at hand? If the student has input into the decision making, this will increase the chances for a successful resolution. Differences of opinion can be acknowledged without being resolved; emphasize the points in common. Focus on possible strategies that will help the student. Ask yourself the following questions: What needs to be done? Are there alternatives from which the child can choose? Who can help? When? Where? How often? Develop a schedule, a time line. Determine the parent's responsibility and the child's responsibility, as well as your own role in reaching desired goals.

Evaluation

Consider how progress will be determined. How will follow-up plans be made to evaluate the results? Make plans for future communication between the parent and teacher. Will you schedule another conference, talk by telephone, or send home a progress report? A follow-up form can be sent home a few days after the meeting asking parents what they learned as a result of the conference, as well as additional thoughts that they might have on issues that were discussed.

Conclusion

Invite each participant to summarize what he or she understands from the conference and what he or she intends to do. You may wish to write down a list of points or have the student take notes to review aloud. Thank the parent for sharing information with you and for planning for the child's success in school. Ask for feedback on what you can do to be most helpful in the future.

The Reviews

After the conference has been completed, spend some time reflecting on your performance and noting areas for improvement.

- Did you help the parent feel comfortable?
- Were you able to answer the parent's questions?
- Did you give the parent time to speak, or did you do most of the talking?
- Did you emphasize the student's strengths as well as his or her weaknesses?
- Did you keep the conference focused on the student and not the parent or the school?
- Was a plan developed?
- Were important points summarized?
- Does each person know his or her responsibility?
- Was there anything you forgot to mention that you would like to include next time?

It will be helpful for you to summarize the main points of the conference for your own records as a reference for progress and a reminder of what transpired before the next scheduled meeting. You may want to create a journal of conference notes in a book or on index cards for easy filing.

WHEN THINGS DON'T GO AS PLANNED

Even the most experienced teachers have difficulties at times. Parents are not always as cooperative and pleasant as we would like them to be. Single parents and working parents, for example, find it difficult to schedule appointments. If a parent brings his or her own personal problems to the conference, they might take priority over the problems of the child. The parent may need a sounding board before he or she can look at the problems of the child. Sometimes, interactions become heated and tempers flare. There may also be some resentment toward the teacher as an authority figure or a representative of an institution viewed as repressive or uncaring. For these and other reasons, you will encounter parents who appear less interested in helping their child than they do in knocking you for a loop.

You may find yourself dealing with difficult parents who are either frightened and defensive or extremely aggressive and demanding. We will review examples and discuss strategies for working with such challenging parents.

The Parent Who Is Angry

"My daughter does not cheat, and I resent you implying such a filthy lie!" Larisa had attempted to take a vocabulary test with the help of a "cheat sheet."

The teacher must recognize that anger is often due to frustration. The best approach in this situation is to let the parent vent his or her feelings while maintaining an accepting attitude. You will need to use your listening skills and empathic attitude. This will be very hard to do because you will also be feeling angry for having your integrity questioned. Self-control, however, will serve you well. Use your reflection and listening skills until the anger loses its momentum. Don't argue; that will only aggravate matters.

Change the focus of the discussion to one of problem solving in which you attempt to enlist the parent's help in resolving the difficulties. A general rule to keep in mind during any interpersonal struggle is this: When you are doing something that doesn't work, don't do it anymore; try something else. If trying to change the parent's mind isn't successful, rather than redoubling your efforts, try backing off instead. Try anything other than what isn't working. But do not, under any circumstances, let things escalate into a shouting match. Inner tranquility can best be maintained if you talk to yourself throughout the encounter, reminding yourself that this isn't personal, that the parent is just doing the best he or she can, and that nothing will be gained by trying to humiliate him or her.

Naturally, you must draw the line if the parent becomes disrespectful or abusive. At that point, suggest that a colleague or administrator join you as mediator. Rescheduling an appointment at another time is also effective because the parent will have had time to regain composure.

We give you fair warning that no matter how conciliatory, easygoing, and nonconfrontational you may be, there may come a time when a parent will jump all over you for no legitimate reason that you can identify. Try to prepare yourself for such an encounter in advance so that you are not so surprised that you cannot gather your wits and act professionally. Bring the session to a close as gracefully as you can.

The Parent Who Is Disappointed

"I don't know what I can do," said Mrs. Cohen. She was disappointed that her son had received a D on his report card. *"He's such a good boy. We had such high hopes for him, but he just doesn't seem to care about school."*

Parents can sabotage their children just as much by being overinvolved as by being neglectful. Some children feel a tremendous sense of power in being able to say to their parents, "You can't make me do anything that I don't want to do. And just to prove it, I will do the opposite of what you want."

Some parents also have unrealistic expectations for their children. Regardless of the child's interests or talents, the parents press him or her to live out their own aspirations. This is also likely to result in disappointment.

Parents who are disappointed need someone who will hear them out. You can be of invaluable assistance by helping them to do a "reality check," comparing what they expect versus what is possible. You can also help them to understand the degree to which they are imposing their own goals on their children, who may have agendas of their own. Finally, you can help them sort out what they may be doing to contribute to the disappointing results. Applying the strategy we mentioned in the previous section, a parent was helped to realize that nagging his child to do homework not only decreased the likelihood that it would be completed but actually guaranteed that the child would rebel. By backing off a bit, the child was given the freedom to assume more responsibility for his own life rather than feeling as if he was always disappointing his father.

The Parent Who Is Troubled

"Jenny is just getting to be too much for me to handle. With all the things that have happened to me lately, I just can't seem to concentrate very well. I know Jenny needs my help, but sometimes I just can't find the energy."

The parent who is troubled needs someone outside his or her circle of family and friends to listen. In some situations, you will be viewed as a professional who is both compassionate and highly skilled—and you can do a lot for someone who is troubled by helping that person feel understood. In most circumstances, however, your main task is to develop enough trust in your relationship with the troubled parent that he or she will respect your advice to get help from a professional. Depressed, anxious, or otherwise suffering parents are in no position to help their children. Your job is to urge them to consult a professional therapist or physician, if not for their own good, then certainly for the benefit of children who are being shortchanged.

The task of encouraging someone to seek professional help is not as easy as it sounds: People who are experiencing emotional difficulties are often resistant to the idea of seeing a mental health professional because of fears that they will be labeled as "crazy." You can pave the way for parents by guiding them to address their concerns and then firmly encouraging them to follow through with their resolve. You may have a list of parent organizations that offer support. They may find reassurance in the fact that other parents are struggling with the same issues.

The Parent Who Is Manipulative

"I know you said on the phone that you wouldn't change my daughter's grade, and I certainly respect your professional judgment in these matters, but . . ."

Not all the parents you meet will be straightforward as to what they want from you; some will have hidden agendas that involve getting you to do things you don't want to do or feel uncomfortable doing. The issue of changing grades is just one example. Others may include the parent who wants you to give special preference to his or her child. Another may want you to make unreasonable arrangements or to accommodate inappropriate requests.

The intrinsic conflict in these situations is that some parents want something from you. They know that if the request is put to you directly, you will say no. So, they resort to manipulative, devious, or underhanded ways to get their way. Some of these parents will attempt to intimidate you by exploiting their power ("I have a good friend on the School Board") or by threatening you ("I just may have to initiate disciplinary action against you if you persist in being so close-minded about this").

There are no easy answers for dealing with parents who are manipulative. We mention this circumstance more as a warning to you than as a situation that has definite solutions. We simply urge you to stand by your professional standards and not give in to manipulative ploys. But you must recognize what is happening before it is too late. Such awareness comes from experience.

Good supervision and support also are crucial, especially for you in the early part of your career not only in learning the ins and outs of conducting parent conferences but in all facets of your work. When you encounter these parents, you will need someone in your corner—your principal, a mentor, a senior colleague, someone who can lend support and advise you how to make it through the traps that have been set.

The Parent Who Is Quiet

This individual can be one of the most challenging parents with whom to make contact in a conference. Because of nervousness, uncertainty about what is expected, limited English fluency, or just a passive personality, some parents will sit throughout the conference and barely say a word.

Families from various cultures may remain relatively quiet in the presence of teachers. You may find yourself babbling to fill the time and then feel very uncomfortable about what took place.

What to do with a parent who is quiet depends very much on why the person is reticent. Therefore, your first assignment should be to try to make such a determination: "I notice that you are not saying very much." The parent will then clarify that he feels a little uncomfortable, or that he doesn't know what you expect, or that he just doesn't talk much. (You can verify the last assumption if he replies to your statement by saying, "Yup.")

In some instances, language may be a barrier. In this case, it may be helpful to have a school interpreter or another family member on hand. The school culture itself may be totally unfamiliar to some parents. You may meet with parents whose children have never been in school before.

In most cases, being patient so that the parent will come to know and trust you will be enough for the parent to open up a bit. Remember, however, that if you attempt to fill the silences with a nonstop monologue, then the parent will never have the chance to engage with you.

The Parent Who Comes Unannounced

A movement at the window of your door catches your eye. There is an adult you do not recognize at the entrance of your room. When you open the door, a parent introduces herself and requests just a moment of your time to review Rianne's grade point average.

This is not the time for a parent conference. You have responsibilities in the classroom with your students. Even if the students are quietly working on an assignment, it is not appropriate to hold a conference in the presence of the students. You can thank the parent for her concern and request she return at a suitable time when you can meet with her.

Every conference has its own pace and distinct characteristics. If you remain sensitive and responsive to each parent's personality, then you can adapt your style of interaction to fit the unique requirements of the situation. In some conferences, the parent will do most of the talking; in others, you will take more of a direct lead—by giving information and asking questions. The more flexible you can be in the way you conduct conferences, the more likely you will develop positive working relationships with a variety of parents from diverse cultures, backgrounds, and personal situations.

We do not wish to make you unduly apprehensive or mistrustful about the parents you will encounter. The vast majority will be cooperative, respectful, and very grateful for your high degree of dedication and competence. Be warned, however, that about once a semester, you will probably meet at least one parent who will not be very pleasant.

MULTICULTURAL PERSPECTIVES

Flexibility is indeed the key to building trust and respect in your relationships with parents. It requires knowledge of the diverse cultural backgrounds from which your children originate and a willingness on your part to do what it takes to help individuals with different values, needs, and interests feel comfortable. You have already learned the importance of multicultural sensitivity with respect to reaching children; the same principles apply to working with their parents.

You will need to learn about the attitudes and customs of the cultures from which your students come in order to (a) understand the behavior patterns of the children and their parents and (b) avoid problems of miscommunication. In particular, pay attention to nonverbal communication. For example, in many ethnic groups, it is considered rude to make eye contact with an adult. For this reason, people look down rather than at a speaker. Different attitudes toward competition explain why some students will turn to others for help during a test. Cooperation rather than competition may be emphasized at home. Certain cultures frown on women in authoritative roles. Consequently, a female teacher may have difficulty establishing rapport with male parents without knowing why. Developing an appreciation and awareness of the various groups from which your students come will facilitate your interactions with them.

Most parents enjoy hearing positive things about their children. The more information they have on progress, the more supportive they will be of your program and your efforts.

SUGGESTED ACTIVITIES

1. Explore the dynamics of your family history, noting the impact of your parents' conduct on your own behavior at school. Try to recall a specific instance in which something your parents did or said had a dramatic impact on your life. What could a teacher have done to intervene with your parents on your behalf?

2. Recruit a few friends or colleagues to help you role-play a parent conference. Concentrate on applying the helping skills (especially questioning and active listening) during your interaction.

3. With your partners, you take on the role of an angry or defensive parent who feels threatened by the teacher's influence and authority over his or her child. After the interaction, talk about your feelings and reactions from the parent's point of view. What did it feel like to have your competence as a parent challenged?

4. Write a sample letter to parents describing the objectives of a parent-teacher conference. Include what you hope to accomplish, what the

parents might expect to occur, where and when the meeting will take place, and what can be done in preparation.

5. Interview a sample of parents of children of different ages. Ask them what their best and worst experiences have been in conferences with teachers. Solicit their advice about some things that you might do differently.

6. Interview several teachers about their favorite methods of leading parent conferences. Ask how they prepare for the meetings, how they keep themselves in control when they are being challenged, how they keep parents focused on the goals of the meeting, and how they use the time most effectively.

SUGGESTED READING

Arends, R. I. (2007). *Learning to teach.* Boston: McGraw-Hill.

Austin, T. (1994). *Changing the view: Student-led parent conferences.* New York: Heinemann.

Boult, B. (2006). *176 ways to involve parents: Practical strategies for partnering with families.* Thousand Oaks, CA: Corwin Press.

Gorman, J. C. (2004). *Working with challenging parents of students with special needs.* Thousand Oaks, CA: Corwin Press.

Jonson, K. F. (2002). *The new elementary teacher's handbook: Flourishing in your first year* (2nd ed.). Thousand Oaks, CA: Corwin Press.

McEwan, E. K. (2004). *How to deal with parents who are angry, troubled, afraid, or just plain crazy.* Thousand Oaks, CA: Corwin Press.

Picciotto, L. P. (1996). *Student-led parent conferences.* New York: Scholastic Books.

Rudney, G. L. (2005). *Every teacher's guide to working with parents.* Thousand Oaks, CA: Corwin Press.

Rutherford, P. (2002). *Why didn't I learn this in college?* Alexandria, VA: Just Ask Publications.

Simpson, R. L. (1996). *Working with parents and families of exceptional children and youth: Techniques for successful conferencing and collaboration* (3rd ed.). Austin, TX: Pro-Ed.

Consulting Effectively With Other Professionals

7

No matter how knowledgeable and skilled you are in the counseling process; no matter how comfortable and adept you become in the various roles you play; no matter how proficiently you are able to communicate with others, assess children's problems, understand their underlying issues, and design effective helping strategies—you will still need the assistance of a number of other professionals and specialists in your work. The best teachers functioning in counseling roles are, in fact, those who can diagnose accurately that a problem exists and know where and to whom to turn for expert guidance.

Teachers not only serve as consultants to others, such as parents and children, but they often solicit the services of experts when they require specialized help. You will ask for outside assistance for several reasons:

- To gain the benefit of expertise that is outside your specialty
- To help you look at fresh or innovative solutions to problems you face
- To get a more detached and objective perspective on what you are experiencing
- To get help handling tasks that you do not have the time or inclination to complete
- To provide you with training in a particular area of need
- To provide you with a multicultural perspective that you are lacking

Once you walk into a school building, you will find that you are not alone. You will be surrounded by people who will likely go out of their way to help you—your fellow teachers. Immediately, you will have the opportunity to network with people teaching the same grade or subject area as you are. In a large school, the head of the department will serve as a resource person for you.

CONSULTING WITH A MENTOR

Many schools will match you with a mentor who may be the department head or an experienced colleague. A mentor will guide you through the maze of school routines, procedures, rituals, and papers to be filled out. Such a person can also assist you when you are confronted with student problems that seem beyond your training and expertise. It is always a good idea to consult with a colleague you trust when you feel in over your head, as you will inevitably feel on occasion when students approach you with their concerns and problems.

Many districts have formal induction programs for teachers new to the school and/or some type of a beginning teacher program in which support providers meet with participating teachers on a regular basis in a series of professional development activities. The mentor-protégé relationship will sustain you in times of stress and provide someone with whom to celebrate your accomplishments. Good mentors provide emotional support for and understanding of your experiences.

Mentors can help you focus and reflect in a collaborative way. In a consulting conference, once you have identified a problem or concern, the two of you will explore the topic presented, examine the possibilities, and identify one for you to try. Later, you'll meet to follow up on what happened and reflect on the results.

Keep in mind that with the training you have just received related to counseling skills for teachers, you may know a lot more than many others about effective ways to help troubled children.

CONSULTING WITH OTHER TEACHERS

Other teachers are available to give assistance as well. They will help you put crises in perspective, show you the tricks of the trade, give you background on students if you want it, and explain school traditions.

> *"Boogie," said the 6'2" football player after the teacher called the name Thomas Barlett, III, on the first day of school.*
>
> *"Boogie?" the teacher repeated with confusion. She had asked the students to tell her what name they preferred to be called. "Boogie," he affirmed.*
>
> *This was a nickname the teacher was not too sure about. So, she went to one of the coaches after school, who explained that everyone called the young man Boogie, and that there was no need for concern.*

As you develop relationships with other personnel in the school, including custodians, librarians, hall monitors, and secretaries, you will find many people to whom to turn and people who will turn to you.

Mindy had developed a negative attitude in her geography class after neglecting to study for a test and failing it. Her choir was going on a two-day trip to perform in a competition, and her teacher was concerned that Mindy would get behind in her classwork and that her attitude would deteriorate further. When Mindy asked her teacher to sign a release from class, the teacher deferred doing so for a day in order to speak to the choir director about the situation. The two teachers decided to talk to Mindy together regarding her behavior and grades in geography. Mindy admitted that she hadn't studied and promised to make time for homework. She also agreed to complete the assignments she would be missing before the field trip so that when she returned, she would be at the same point as the rest of the class.

Many schools have a policy that a student's participation in extracurricular activities depends on his or her maintaining certain grades or a certain grade point average. So, if a student's behavior or grades are becoming questionable, speak to the band director, club sponsor, coach, or whoever sponsors the activity to see if you can work together to help the student.

Your fellow teachers, especially those who have just completed their first year, have a wealth of experience from which to draw. Whether you have questions about discipline, implementation of the curriculum, or ordering supplies, or if you just need to talk about a bad day, these people can be a support system for you.

CONSULTING WITH THE PRINCIPAL

Administrators can also be a tremendous source of inspiration, support, and guidance. They are mentors in the truest sense of having someone in your corner whose main function is to make your job easier.

Perhaps one of your greatest challenges is to develop a working relationship with the administrator who evaluates your work so that you will feel comfortable when situations arise that are difficult for you. Relationships such as these are not built overnight; trust accrues slowly. Of course, you can help the process along rather than wait for the other person to make overtures. Invite the principal to stop by your room to see projects that the students have created or a bulletin board you put up as a teaching aid. Invite him or her to participate in a class activity. This tactic offers the principal an opportunity to get involved in your domain, and it also lets him or her know what is going on in your classroom. Speak to the principal on a positive note, giving feedback, for example, on an assembly that went smoothly, or an extracurricular activity, or a staff development session that you found particularly meaningful. Report on the progress of committee work. Approach him or her with an idea or suggestion for improvement.

School administrators are expert problem solvers. Let them know when you need assistance. Remember, they were in your shoes once.

They are familiar with the frustrations of teaching, although they may need to be reminded of the specific difficulties you experience in your field. Whether your school becomes the best place you have ever worked or a land mine of potential obstacles and dangers depends to a large part on the relationships you forge with administrators and department heads. Whether in industry or education, developing a relationship with a supervisor who could potentially become a caring mentor is crucial for job satisfaction and success within the system.

MAKING A REFERRAL

Even in those cases when you are fairly certain that the nature of the problem is beyond the scope of what you can handle, given the already heavy demands on your time and energy, you will still want to get the helping process rolling. Even when you know that a child needs help and have identified the appropriate professional to whom to refer, there is still some uncertainty as to whether the child (and/or his or her family) will ever show up. The act of making a referral thus requires a great deal of tact and skill to increase the likelihood that help will take place. This is far more likely if several conditions are met:

1. You have developed a good relationship with the child so that he or she feels your concern, caring, and commitment.

2. You understand the nature of how counseling works and have begun the process in such a way that help is likely to continue.

3. You have helped the child set realistic expectations and goals for what counseling can and can't do.

4. You have applied some basic listening and responding skills so that the child has a good experience in a counseling-type relationship and is therefore more amenable to continuing such a relationship with a professional.

5. You secure a commitment from the child to do something about his or her situation.

6. You make consistent efforts to follow up on the referral to make sure the child did seek help as promised.

Each of these steps can be implemented if you understand the way the counseling process operates. This includes grasping the stages of what usually takes place as well as the skills that are involved along the way. Whether you are applying the most rudimentary counseling skills in preparation for a referral or are taking someone through the complete process yourself, you will follow the same principles presented previously.

CONSULTING WITH COUNSELORS

It was hard for Mr. Blane to describe the changes he had noticed in Teresa. She was maybe a little quieter, a bit more pensive than usual. She still did her work and participated in class discussions, but something was different about her energy level. He could not quite put his finger on it. Mr. Blane's attempts to communicate with her were quickly cut off. "How's it going?" was answered with the typical, "Fine." "How are you today?" "Good." End of conversation. He decided to visit the girl's counselor and ask her if she would discreetly talk to the girl.

A few days later, the counselor reported that there were indeed some problems in the family, things that Teresa preferred remain confidential. The counselor expressed gratitude for Mr. Blane's perceptive observations and reassured him that everything was once again under control. Mr. Blane was still intensely curious about what had happened with Teresa and her family, but the counselor explained that sometimes children prefer to talk to someone other than their teacher. In this case, because Teresa liked Mr. Blane so much, she did not want him to know anything about her that did not show her in the best light. Sometimes it happens that although we want to be helpful to students, our authority role prevents us from developing the kind of relationship that counselors are perfectly positioned and trained to create.

When you can't seem to establish rapport with a particular student or the situation is too much for you to handle, counselors can provide the support and guidance you need. What will you do when you suspect a child is being abused or neglected? What about when a child approaches you for advice about using birth control? How will you handle the situation when you notice an abrupt change in a child's personality? Counselors can provide support, feedback, and problem-solving skills. They can help you address issues of self-esteem and career education, or they can work directly with your students. They can teach communication skills, decision-making skills, the development of self-control, cooperation skills, emotional control, and the ability to laugh at oneself rather than take oneself too seriously. They can lead self-help groups (with you as a coleader, if you like). Furthermore, they can provide you and your students with resources in the community.

Sometimes, you may consult with a counselor informally, such as in the case of Mr. Blane. Other times, it may be best to handle the situation yourself with the guidance of the counselor. In either instance, counselors can be your best resources in addressing the emotional needs of your students and yourself.

SEEING A COUNSELOR AS YOUR PERSONAL CONSULTANT

A unique feature of counseling as a profession is that a person does not need to have an emotional disorder or even a problem to seek help. Whereas other mental health professionals such as psychiatrists, psychologists, and social workers specialize in treating severe mental disorders, counselors are experts in helping people with normal concerns of daily living. This includes, but is not limited to, having adjustment problems, making life changes, developing one's career, finding meaning in one's life, developing better self-understanding, resolving relationship difficulties, planning for the future, reducing stress, or dealing with any other struggle that human beings face as a part of daily existence.

Although teaching is a very rewarding profession, it is also a stressful one—filled with demands, responsibilities, and commitments that sometimes seem beyond what any person could reasonably be expected to handle. As an authority figure, you will be a target for some children who wish to act out their frustration and hostility. Sometimes, you will be caught in a tug-of-war between administrators, parents, and children, with no apparent escape in sight. Furthermore, the burnout rate in teaching is high because of what is expected from you.

Deciding to seek the services of a counselor (perhaps being referred by the counselor in your school) as your personal consultant can therefore help you in a number of ways:

1. An experience as a client can help you improve your own helping skills. By watching a professional at work, by noting what works best for you, you will find yourself unconsciously and deliberately adapting strategies to your own situations.

2. You will have a safe, confidential support system that will give you the opportunity to work through stresses and concerns without having to burden your family and friends.

3. You can motivate yourself to grow and to continue learning about those aspects of your functioning that you wish to improve.

4. You can work through particular difficulties that crop up in your life. Issues that teachers are especially vulnerable to include a fear of failure, feelings of uncertainty as to whether the rewards of the profession are worth the aggravation, feelings of stagnation, and conflicts with colleagues or administrators.

5. You can counteract the deleterious effects of classroom life. On a regular basis, you will be dealing with children who do not necessarily want to be within your control or domain; some will fight you every

inch of the way. The wear and tear takes its toll until, eventually, you will start to feel serious effects—unless, of course, you have developed coping skills to help you stay energized.

Many of these reasons for consulting a counselor are evident in the testimony of one beginning teacher who did quite well in her teacher education program yet encountered a number of adjustment difficulties her first year on the job:

> *I really had no idea how hard it would be for me to finish this first school year. Several times, I wanted to quit. In fact, I probably would have quit if I hadn't seen a counselor during some difficult times.*
>
> *I was always so organized at the university. I kept up with my assignments, did what I was told, got good grades. I learned a lot. But I still wasn't adequately prepared for the chaos I would have to deal with— a principal who had a style that was somewhat less than supportive, colleagues who were bickering, kids who showed no interest, parents who cared even less. I was totally demoralized and started to consider other career options.*
>
> *At the suggestion of a friend, I started seeing a counselor recommended to me by one of our school counselors. At first, I didn't much like it at all. I kept it a secret because I thought people might think I was going crazy—actually, that is how it felt to me.*
>
> *But then, it started to feel so good to have somebody I could talk to, someone who didn't judge me or tell me what to do, someone who believed in me, who encouraged me to look at some difficult aspects of myself that I don't much like. I examined the very reasons why I wanted to be a teacher in the first place. I even began to realize that it wasn't just the kids and the parents and the administrators—it was me, too. There were some things that I had been doing to make life more difficult than it needed to be. Wow! It was an amazing experience.*

CONSULTING WITH THE SCHOOL PSYCHOLOGIST

Traditionally, school psychologists have focused most of their attention on testing and assessment of children for placement in special programs. However, as they add consulting to their repertoire of services, they offer a wealth of support and information in many areas, from individual differences in learning styles and classroom dynamics to multicultural needs and effective behavior management strategies. They offer not only expertise in problem solving with individual students, but also prevention services for all students. They can offer programs on a variety of topics such as peer pressure, test anxiety, self-esteem, and loneliness.

Furthermore, they will help you identify students who are at risk and develop programs for them.

When you experience a problem, you will probably feel considerable relief at knowing that you are not alone. In some schools, your first step will be to try to resolve the problem in the classroom. If unsuccessful, next you would present the problem for review to an in-school team consisting of several professionals. Then, if the need still persists, the screening committee will make a formal referral to the school psychologist. In other schools, the school psychologist is available to work with teachers directly. Both situations allow you to access the expertise of a professional trained specifically to assess children's difficulties and to prescribe programs for remediation.

CONSULTING WITH HOMELESS EDUCATION COMMUNITY LIAISONS

As some families may become homeless, medical and school records may be lost. School attendance may become erratic and performance affected. One can only imagine what it must be like to live on the streets or in transit housing without a safe, stable home environment.

Teachers can be aware of signs such as an address of a motel; self-identification of transitional living circumstances; reports of multiple families living together; lack of continuity in education; poor health/nutrition; poor hygiene; transportation problems; concern about personal space after school; social and behavioral concerns; and reaction statements by parent(s), guardian(s), and children. Older children are less likely to identify themselves as homeless as they are concerned with privacy. Teachers and other school personnel must be careful to maintain confidentiality so as to not stigmatize them.

Homeless children frequently need clothing, school supplies, and social services. They and their parents need to be informed of the student's right to stay in the school of origin or local school, providing continuity of relationships and academics. They also have the right to immediate enrollment and transportation provided by the school. As a result of legislation, most school districts have an identified district liaison who advocates for homeless children. The liaison will facilitate the process of enrollment and help students receive the benefits of free or reduced price meals immediately. They will help students get needed immunizations and referrals for other services. The liaison will meet with these students on a regular basis, monitoring attendance and grades.

In the classroom, teachers can provide extra support and attention to help homeless students feel comfortable by assigning buddies to assist with school procedures and routines in the classroom. They can welcome them back to school after absences and help ease their transition back to the class activities by explaining what they missed and making plans to catch up.

CONSULTING WITH FACULTY AT THE LOCAL UNIVERSITY

Education professors, instructors, and supervisors are often quite eager to provide help to teachers who are experiencing difficulties or who simply have questions on how to handle matters. The local university will also serve as a resource for you. You can invite college faculty (with the permission of your principal) to demonstrate the latest educational techniques in your classroom and/or meet with them to critique your teaching style. They are available to do workshops for you and your staff on particular areas of interest, and many would be happy to consult with you regarding methods, materials, behavior management, and other concerns you might have.

The university may also have established groups that meet on a regular basis. Often they hold daylong conferences and offer workshops for teachers in the community. These groups provide opportunities for you to interact with your peers, as well as develop your skills.

One group of teachers in an elementary school was concerned about the high rate of single-parent homes in which their children resided. Because counselors in the district were at a premium, there were very little, if any, services offered to address this growing problem. The teachers approached their principal to see if she would support their intent to begin support groups for children experiencing problems adjusting to the separation of their parents. Together, they decided to recruit the assistance of faculty at the university, who trained them in the skills and methods of developing such a program. Once the groups began, the counselor education faculty remained available to provide ongoing supervision.

THE TEACHER'S ROLE IN INDIVIDUALIZED EDUCATION PROGRAMS

The teacher is an active participant in the development of the individualized education program (IEP) for a special education student. Having already consulted with the school psychologist, the teacher will also confer with the child's parent(s). Often, it is the teacher who becomes aware that a problem exists. It is the teacher who usually first contacts the parent(s). It is the teacher who arranges for testing. As an advocate for the student, the teacher finds him- or herself a central figure in working with the resource teachers, school psychologists, and parents as coordinator and disseminator of information. The teacher may be the only person present at the conference who knows everybody.

In particular, the teacher must be sensitive to the emotions and concerns of the parent(s). When parents are informed that a child may qualify for special help, they typically experience a pattern of reactions: shock, denial, guilt, anger, and/or frustration. Other parents may express great relief that someone is finally paying attention to their child and providing the help sorely needed. Of the people participating in an initial IEP, the teacher may be the only person with whom the parents have had contact. Therefore, parents may seek out teachers for answers to questions and for emotional support.

One of the first considerations is to inform parents of the nature of the proceeding itself. They need to know who will be participating, where the meeting will be held, and how long it will last. The teacher can be helpful in explaining the terminology that will be used. The teacher can request that all reports of testing be sent to the parent ahead of time. Often, a pre-conference with the parents is advised to answer any questions and explain the types of questions that will be asked. At this time, information can be solicited from the parents with respect to the child's developmental history, school history, and attitudes from the parents' perspective. This preconference meeting will help foster a positive rapport between the family and the school and set a cooperative tone for the IEP itself.

At the IEP meeting, assessments will be analyzed and interpreted. Then, a specific plan will be developed for the forthcoming year. The parents will need to have explained how the plan will be specifically implemented. They will want to know what is expected of them. They will want to know the details of scheduling, times, locations, and transportation, if appropriate. They will want to know which instructional approaches and behavioral strategies will be used. The parents will continue to need the support of the teacher who can help them maintain a positive outlook. The teacher can emphasize the strengths of the student and point out where and how to look for progress in the future.

TEACHERS ARE NOT COUNSELORS

Although in this chapter, and throughout this book, we have spoken to you about those situations in which you will be using counseling skills, you have not had the specialized training (usually the equivalent of two to three years of full-time study—a 60-credit master's degree) to be counselors. The skills we have presented and the knowledge base we have introduced are only a rudimentary background to help you prepare better for the multiple roles you will play in your profession.

Unfortunately, in spite of your best intentions to address all the needs of your students—psychological as well as academic—you will just not have the time to do the complete job that you would prefer. Your hands will be more than full keeping up with your instructional responsibilities and the support activities that go along with them. Nevertheless, we have shown you a number of ways to integrate counseling methods and skills into your interpersonal style and classroom environment. We have helped you to feel comfortable in referring students to appropriate professionals for guidance and counseling.

What would you like your students to say about you 10 years from now? How would you most like to be remembered by all the kids with whom you will come into contact throughout your career? It would be nice if they remembered that you taught them some important things about life, the world, and themselves. But even more fulfilling—imagine that they'll say you really cared about them. You were there for them, really there. They will remember that you were a great listener, someone whom they could trust. You were someone who saw them as individuals. You did not judge them, nor did you criticize them (even though you were critical of their problematic behavior). They will remember that to you, teaching was not just a job. It was not just something that you did. A teacher is who you were. A teacher is who you are.

SUGGESTED ACTIVITIES

1. Answer the following questions in a journal or small group discussion: Who were the teachers who inspired you the most in your life? What were they like, and what did they do that made the most difference to you?

2. How would you most like to be remembered as a teacher? If a group of your former students were to meet 20 years from now and talk about you, what would you like them to say?

3. Interview a school counselor, a school psychologist, a university professor, and an administrator to find out how they perceive their roles as consultants to teachers.

4. Make a list of the situations, problems, and concerns that you feel least prepared to deal with. Start building a resource file of experts in the community with whom you could consult about those situations. Compile a list of resources and support groups that are also available.

5. Based on the topics we have covered in this book, and what you have learned, make a commitment to follow through on three resolutions that you believe are important to your role as a teacher. Share them in a group or write them down.

SUGGESTED READING

Blase, J., & Blase, J. J. (2006). *Teachers bringing out the best in teachers: A guide to peer consultation for administrators and teachers.* Thousand Oaks, CA: Corwin Press.

Brigman, G., Mullis, F., Webb, L., & White, J. F. (2004). *School counselor consultation: Skills for working effectively with parents, teachers, and other school personnel.* New York: John Wiley.

Portner, H. (2002). *Being mentored: A guide for protégés.* Thousand Oaks, CA: Corwin Press.

Shulman, J. H., & Sato, M. T. (2006). *Mentoring teachers toward excellence: Supporting and developing highly qualified teachers.* San Francisco: Jossey-Bass.

Counseling
Yourself

8

O ne of the most fantastic benefits of learning counseling skills is that they work as well for you as they do with others. It is virtually impossible to listen to someone else's struggles without personalizing similar problems that you have encountered. Likewise, through the altruistic act of helping others resolve difficulties, you almost can't help but do the same for yourself.

It will not surprise you to hear that becoming more responsive and empathic in your relationships with students also changes your personal relationships for the better. Professional therapists and counselors often report that, during those times when they are challenging their clients to let go of their dysfunctional thinking and self-defeating behaviors, they are far more likely to do so in their own lives as well.

Most of the skills you have learned in this book involve being more compassionate with others; this works just as well in being more forgiving of yourself. Most of the skills encourage you to listen and respond more effectively with students, a strategy that will serve you well in enhancing all your relationships. You have learned to make better sense of your students' behavior, what they are communicating by their actions; this analytic style will also assist you in efforts to unravel puzzling and conflicting interactions in your personal life. Finally, when students are feeling stressed or out of control, you have learned ways to help them regain a sense of balance. These strategies can do the same for you as well—if you apply them on a regular basis and practice what you preach to others.

We have covered elsewhere the power of modeling, that is, how students learn not just from what we say but also what we do. When students observe us working through issues in constructive ways, and they admire the results that accrue, they feel even more motivated to follow our leads. I (Jeffrey) remember a time when I was teaching our son to throw a ball at a target. Every time I missed, I would involuntarily mutter to myself, "Damn!" Before long, I noticed that he was doing the same thing. This little guy, about four years old, was saying "Damn" to himself every time he missed the target. Once that had my attention, I changed what I said out loud to, "That's okay," demonstrating a more forgiving, relaxed attitude. In no time, he was imitating that as well. The lesson was driven home that children (and others) pay close attention to the ways we manage frustration, deal with disappointment, resolve conflicts, and handle distress. They learn as much from watching us as they do from anything that might be part of our cherished lesson plans.

STUDENTS WHO CHANGE YOU

A student complains to you of feeling lonely and misunderstood and that triggers thoughts about the relative superficiality of some of your friendships.

A student comes to you in tears because she has been teased for being overweight. Even if you don't have a problem yourself with body image, it still might provoke you to think of taking better care of yourself.

Two students are working together on a group project and you recognize their troubles trying to perform perfectly. This reminds you of your own unresolved issues related to perfectionism and always falling short.

In class one day, you notice a student who seems unusually disengaged and lethargic. You picture yourself at that age and are immediately reminded of difficult times you lived through.

Each of these examples becomes an opportunity for you to become more reflective about your life and where you are headed. Each conversation you have with a child about something bothering him or her forces you to look at yourself in a different light. Each helping encounter produces reciprocal effects in which you may be changed as much as the student.

Relationships between teachers and students involve an interesting collaboration. Although we are the ones who are trained and paid as experts, it is not unusual that we can learn as much from students as they learn from us. In one study of this reciprocal change process, I (Jeffrey) interviewed the most famous therapists on the planet, asking them to look back on their distinguished careers and pick out the one client who had the most impact on them as professionals and persons. In other words, think about all the people you have helped during your life and career. Who stands out as being the one student (or person) who taught you the most? We are not just referring to what he or she taught you about being a better teacher, but also a more effective person.

Based on these interviews, and other research on reciprocal change in helping relationships, there are a few key themes that are worth mentioning.

1. Great educators view their students as teachers. They are open to what others can teach them. They refine their methods based on closely monitoring what others tell them (verbally and by their behavior) about what works best and what does not. They also learn a lot about the world, about different cultures and experiences, and about themselves, by being privileged to get to know others.

2. What keeps teachers vitalized and continually growing is the modesty that accompanies an open mind. Students are experts on their own experience. They appreciate being treated with respect, sensitivity, and humility. They also are flattered by the idea that we want to learn from them.

3. The students we remember most vividly are not just the ones who gave us trouble but also the ones who let us get close to them. Relationships are what sustain them—and us as well.

SELF-TALK

Just as we teach students to talk to themselves differently about disappointments, discouragements, and conflicts, we can do the same inside our own minds whenever we face distressing circumstances. Among all the techniques introduced in this book to help others, there is none that is more easily and usefully applied to counseling ourselves. For each of the following internal statements, captured from within a teacher's head, imagine how the irrational, distorted thinking could be altered to represent a more measured, realistic response. Compare the two alternative thought choices to the same, identical stimulus.

Exaggerating

"This sort of thing *always* happens to me. I *never* get what I want" *versus* " It's disappointing that I didn't get what I want this time."

"It's *terrible* that I have such a large, unruly class" *versus* "It's challenging, and even annoying that I have a class larger than what I prefer."

Note the differences in the second statements, how the teacher keeps the disappointing situation in perspective. Clearly it is an exaggeration to think to yourself that you never get what you want or that this is the worst thing that ever happened. Extreme negative, emotional responses result from such distorted thinking.

Absolute Demands

"It isn't fair that the principal gave me such a lousy schedule. He *shouldn't* be this way" *versus* "It is *unfortunate* that I have a schedule that is not ideal. Sometimes I don't believe my principal operates the way I *prefer."*

"Students just don't work as hard as they used to. I just don't think their parents care any more" *versus* "Students and parents seem to behave differently in some ways than they used to. This may be a function of my outlook as much as their behavior."

It is a setup for disappointment and discouragement to make demands that others live up to your expectations and values when they may operate according to different rules or within another cultural context. It is one thing for you to have strong preferences about how others ought to behave (usually the way you would), but it is quite another thing to demand that the world comply with your wishes. Not only are you likely to be repeatedly disappointed but you will also encounter a lot of resistance.

Overgeneralizing

"Because this class gave me a hard time today, they're going to be tough all semester" *versus* "Although this could be a challenging group based on what I observed today, though things could easily change as we get to know one another."

"Maybe I'm not cut out to be a teacher because of the poor way I handled things" *versus* "Sometimes I don't handle things as perfectly as I could, but that does not reflect on my essential competence."

These examples illustrate the differences between language that is externally based, meaning that it focuses on self-talk that blames circumstances beyond your control, as opposed to internal thinking that demonstrates responsibility for your own thoughts and feelings. One of the things you learn when working with children is to challenge not only what they do on the outside but also how they think on the inside about what happens to them. This implies that emotional reactions are choices based on particular interpretations.

There are several ways that you can remind yourself (and others) to use more constructive internal language, especially when you feel upset:

- Avoid the use of *shoulds* and *musts,* which make absolute demands of the world and others based on your preferences
- Stop yourself from imagining the worst possible scenario and instead think about positive outcomes

- Look for exceptions for when you are experiencing problems rather than focusing only on when things go wrong
- Live in the present rather than dwelling in the past
- Ask yourself, "Where is the evidence?"
- Keep expectations realistic to minimize disappointment
- Monitor what you say
- Reframe problems to make them more manageable
- Stop whining and complaining about things you can't control
- Keep your sense of humor and stop taking yourself so seriously
- Watch your tendency to overgeneralize

Externalized Language	Internalized Language
"That student made me so angry."	*"I made myself angry over what he did."*
"It's not my fault. I can't help it."	*"I chose to behave in this way."*
"The class observation made me so nervous."	*"I made myself nervous over the observation."*
"That guy really gets under my skin."	*"I allow that guy to get under my skin."*

Keeping a Thought Journal

The theory underlying self-talk (and the cognitive therapy you learned in Chapter 5) is that most negative emotional reactions are not caused by external events but rather by your interpretations of them. You can choose how to react to almost any situation you face, no matter how challenging or stressful, based on the ways you decide to think about it. In order to help students learn to do this, you have to become skilled and experienced with the process yourself.

One way to teach yourself to become more vigilant and proactive with respect to your thinking involves keeping a *thought journal*, a repository where you can monitor those situations that create the most distress and then unravel how you characteristically think in such predicaments. This should be a notebook or journal that is small enough that you can keep it with you at all times, dutifully recording those situations in which you feel the most out of control.

As the entry in this thought journal illustrates, this beginning teacher is greatly exaggerating and overgeneralizing his situation, blowing it way out of proportion to reality. Sure, it is disappointing to receive an evaluation that is less than stellar, and certainly it merits reflection (and perhaps some changes in method), but what makes this such a crisis in this

Situation	Feelings	Automatic Thoughts
Context and setting	One-word descriptors	What were you thinking just before and during the unpleasant experience?
I received an evaluation on my teaching that was only satisfactory when I know I did far better than that. This was an important stage in my tenure evaluation in my school. I've never gotten any evaluation lower than excellent before, so it has me thinking that maybe the principal doesn't like me. There's a lot at stake for me because I really need this job and I like working in this school. I don't want to have to look for another job.	*Depressed*	*I'm in deep trouble now with no hope of pulling myself out.*
	Humilated	*I might as well quit before I get fired. Maybe I should think about another career.*
	Angry	*It isn't fair that this sort of thing is happening to me. Why me?*
	Frustrated	*This is just about the worst thing that could ever happen, and just at a time when I need some support.*
	Anxious	
	Discouraged	*The principal should have given me more direction and help on this. How am I supposed to read her mind about what she wants?*

person's life is the way he chooses to respond. By writing down his thoughts and feelings, as well as sorting out their origin, he can choose an alternative way of reacting that is more realistic and measured and that perhaps can even lead to constructive action—like having a more extended conversation with his principal to discuss his concerns. This is more likely to turn out constructively if he can present himself in a way that he feels calm, open-minded, and eager to receive feedback rather than exhibiting a defensive, resentful attitude.

SELF-CARE ISSUES FOR TEACHERS

Applying counseling skills to your own life involves far more than merely talking to yourself more effectively, or even taking steps to think more constructively during those times when you are most under pressure. We have discussed previously how students learn as much from how you act as they do from what you teach them as part of your planned lessons. They watch the ways you conduct yourself. They collect anecdotes about your life. In some ways, they even pattern themselves after you based on things you do they admire most.

Think back on those teachers whom you liked and respected the most, especially those with whom you enjoyed a good relationship. It is probable that apart from anything they ever taught you about their discipline, you remember detailed, specific things about their lives—the way they dressed, their special interests, perhaps even their food and exercise habits. Modeling healthy lifestyle habits is certainly influential on students, but that is not the only reason we are talking about ways to initiate better self-care strategies.

Given the high rate of teacher burnout, not to mention the chronic stress that is part of the job, it is imperative that you develop ways to nurture and nourish yourself. You are not much good at taking care of others if you can't do so for yourself. There are several areas in which it is worthwhile to do an honest self-assessment and, if indicated, to make needed changes. These are exactly the same sorts of things that you might encourage in your students who were struggling with similar issues.

Physical health is imperative for you to function effectively in your work and your life. Given that obesity is among the most critical health problems in North America today, monitoring what you eat is imperative. The other aspect of taking care of your body involves regular exercise, that is, something you can do virtually every day to keep yourself fit.

Consider the problems that most kids encounter in their lives—body image, friendships, family conflicts, bad habits, drugs and alcohol, depression and anxiety—these are the same things that you may be struggling with as well. It is difficult for you to offer comfort and support, much less guidance, to students when you have not had success dealing with the same issues.

There are limits to what you can do to help yourself, just as there are with respect to trying to assist students in trouble. Just as you would refer someone to an expert when a situation is outside of your professional training, so, too, might you wish to refer yourself to a counselor or therapist during those times when you feel like you're over your head.

In many counselor training programs, students are encouraged, if not expected, to attend counseling sessions as a client. The reasoning for this policy is that it is hard to help someone else if you have not experienced what it is like to sit in the client's chair. Second, as we have been emphasizing, counselors—or professionals functioning in similar helping roles—have an obligation to work on themselves the same ways they might assist others.

This brief introduction to counseling skills for teachers was just the beginning of your training. Just as increasing your proficiency as a teacher is a lifetime commitment, so, too, is learning to be a more responsive listener for your students and the people whom you love the most. There will be opportunities every day, almost every hour, for you to practice what you have learned.

Index

CORWIN PRESS